Lillian Too
Jennifer Too

FORTUNE & FENG SHUI

DOG

2020

KONSEPBOOKS
ASTROLOGY . FENG SHUI . INSPIRATIONS

FORTUNE & FENG SHUI 2020 DOG
by *Lillian Too* and *Jennifer Too*
© 2020 Konsep Lagenda Sdn Bhd

Text © 2020 Lillian Too and Jennifer Too
Photographs and illustrations © Konsep Lagenda Sdn Bhd

The moral right of the authors to be identified as authors of this book has been asserted.

Published by KONSEP LAGENDA SDN BHD (223 855)
Kuala Lumpur 59100 Malaysia

For more Konsep books, go to *www.lillian-too.com* or *www.wofs.com*
To report errors, please send a note to errors@konsepbooks.com
For general feedback, email feedback@konsepbooks.com

Notice of Rights
All rights reserved. No part of this publication may be reproduced, stored in a retrieval system or transmitted in any form, or by any means, electronic, mechanical, photocopying, recording, or otherwise, without the prior written permission of the publisher.
For information on getting permission for reprints and excerpts, contact: permissions@konsepbooks.com

Notice of Liability
The information in this book is distributed on an "As Is" basis, without warranty. While every precaution has been taken in the preparation of the book, neither the author nor Konsep Lagenda shall have any liability to any person or entity with respect to any loss or damage caused or alleged to be caused directly or indirectly by the instructions contained in this book.

ISBN 978-967-329-279-0
Published in Malaysia, September 2019

DOG 2020

BIRTH YEAR	WESTERN CALENDAR DATES	AGE	KUA NUMBER MALES	KUA NUMBER FEMALES
Wood Dog	14 Feb 1934 - 3 Feb 1935	86	3 East Group	3 East Group
Fire Dog	2 Feb 1946 - 21 Jan 1947	74	9 East Group	6 West Group
Earth Dog	18 Feb 1958 - 7 Feb 1959	62	6 West Group	9 East Group
Metal Dog	6 Feb 1970 - 26 Jan 1971	50	3 East Group	3 East Group
Water Dog	25 Jan 1982 - 12 Feb 1983	38	9 East Group	6 West Group
Wood Dog	10 Feb 1994 - 30 Jan 1995	26	6 West Group	9 East Group
Fire Dog	29 Jan 2006 - 17 Feb 2007	14	3 East Group	3 East Group

CONTENTS

CONTENTS

CONTENTS

CHAPTER 1

METAL RAT YEAR 2020 GENERAL OUTLOOK

Metal Rat Year 2020

A quarrelsome year but with hidden good luck

This year of the Metal Rat 2020 is likely to be a quarrelsome one when there will be plenty of verbal sparring between friends, and even more between foes. As a result, misunderstandings flare up more regularly than usual. It is a year that calls for more patience. Laughter is a good way to glide through the year, as humour is the best way of appeasing the #7 star in the middle of the year's feng shui chart.

FENG SHUI CHART 2020

SOUTH

EARTH — FIRE — EARTH

SOUTHEAST	SOUTH	SOUTHWEST
6 Heavenly Star	2 THREE KILLINGS Illness	SCHOLASTIC LUCK 4 Peach Blossom
EAST	**CENTER**	**WEST**
5 WU WANG Five Yellow	7 BURGLARY Violence	9 Completion
NORTHEAST	**NORTH**	**NORTHWEST**
1 Victory Luck	TAI SUI 3 Quarrelsome	8 Prosperity

EAST — WEST

WOOD — METAL

EARTH — WATER — EARTH

NORTH

There are many months when anger energies get doubled, which indicates the feng shui energies of the world experience an intensity of extremes; and with the #7 star so dominant, it is a year when effort needs to be made to stay calm and collected. Do NOT give in to irritations and annoyances.

GOOD LEADERSHIP IN 2020

But there is good news. Because we see also that those steering the destinies of the world benefit hugely from the #8 star, which flies into the sector of the Northwest.

> We can see that leaders, CEOs and all the patriarchs of the world who make decisions are less prone to succumbing to anger energies – because they benefit from the power of 8, which suggests good leadership skills.

This should ensure the ship that sails in 2020 enjoys having a captain likely to enjoy excellent winds and waters. It is a year when many benefit from stability and good governance. Patriarchs and leaders are likely to be calm and stable in their decision-making, benefitting those who come under their leadership and influence.

IMPORTANT TO NOT LOSE YOUR TEMPER

We need to be wary of impatience in 2020. The #7 as the dominant star number will be the cause of many succumbing to bad temper, irritation and tantrums. The feng shui chart of the year 2020 being ruled by the number 7 is indicative of violence breaking out, as a result of which the year will see a preponderance of discordant energies. The #3 star in the North meanwhile, which is in residence in the Rat sector, makes this Rat year a quarrelsome one, further suggesting that misunderstandings and conflict energies hold sway.

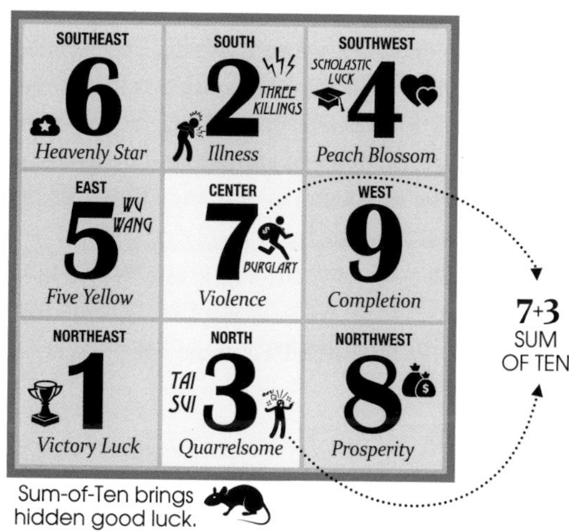

HIDDEN GOOD LUCK

But... there are subtle benefits because implicit within the combination of #7 and #3 is the auspicious sum-of-ten combination. This indicates that hidden beneath misunderstandings and anger energies, a greater aspiration for harmonious completion prevails.

The SUM-OF-TEN always suggests excellent completion luck, good outcomes arising from initial intolerance and afflicted energies, suggesting that "all's well that ends well".

This is the hidden benefit of any sum-of-ten combination, when we can actually experience a bad start afflicted by misunderstanding transforming into good vibrations as a result of other factors coming in to play. Outcomes of conflict and quarrels can therefore be satisfactorily settled, with silver linings behind every cloud. There is no need to worry too much then when arguments and misunderstandings take place. Just go with the flow and let the energies play out. Things will have a way of resolving themselves.

NEW CALENDAR CYCLE

In 2020, the world gets ready to embark on a NEW calendar cycle, the start of a new 60 years, and even a new 180 years. We stand poised to welcome a NEW AGE, which we are already seeing and experiencing. The world has gone digital. We are ruled by energies that are quantum, and the strength of chi is exponentially greater as a result.

We need to expand the horizons of our aspirations and be prepared for new ideas that arise from seemingly nowhere, because creativity will also be at a new height.

Many will allow their imaginations to guide them into new directions of creativity. And because it is a Rat year, these ideas are likely to incorporate the flow of inherent prosperity which can be exploited. People on the lookout for creative new ways to grow their commercial ideas are likely to benefit from the year's energies.

> 2020 is a year when we benefit from broadening our goals to reach beyond ordinary ambitions.

This is a year when we will benefit if we indulge in "quantum thinking", which means going beyond our ordinary expectations. We must not let ourselves be boxed in. We can reach beyond space and time because at the start of this new calendar cycle, we are on the brink of many new breakthroughs.

FENG SHUI BECOMING MORE RELEVANT

This is also a year when feng shui will become increasingly relevant, as many have now been exposed to this ancient way of looking at chi energies. The current digital age has helped disseminate this ancient knowledge to so many, and now the chi energies of the world are moving, reacting and responding at quantum speed. Thus we see energies react faster. Activities that we start will take off more quickly.

We will find that good and bad flows and accumulations of energy manifest at unprecedented speed.

Feng shui is the practice of living in harmony with the winds and waters of the world, and now these seem to be blowing faster and gathering greater strength. This correspondingly means they bring change to our luck and our well-being a lot more rapidly than before.

We are moving into an age when the winds and waters are blowing stronger and faster than ever. As we do, changes to our luck and well-being also happen more rapidly than ever before.

THE FENG SHUI CHART OF 2020

When we look at the Feng Shui Chart of 2020, we see that the dominant number in the center of the chart is 7, which is a Metal number. The element of the ruling number strengthens the energy of the WEST sector this year because METAL is the ruling element of the West.

In 2020, the element of METAL stands for wealth and financial success; thus take note that the center

number being a Metal number spells underlying wealth luck for the year.

MONKEY & ROOSTER BENEFIT FROM WEALTH

Note that the Monkey and Rooster have links to the West sector, hence they benefit from wealth luck due to the strength of the Metal element in the 2020 chart. These two signs can proceed to do whatever they wish to start this year, and it will be financially viable, and with success more than likely to be the result.

The Monkey and Rooster signs benefit from wealth luck in 2020.

Those married to either of these signs or having siblings of these signs can benefit by supporting them in any venture! The Monkey and Rooster are likely to initiate ventures that can create new wealth for their families.

But within the number 7 lies red, which when associated with Metal can indicate bloodshed. The year is thus likely to experience rumblings of violent energy threatening to erupt. It is beneficial thus to make extra effort to be patient and to exercise greater diplomacy in dealings with others.

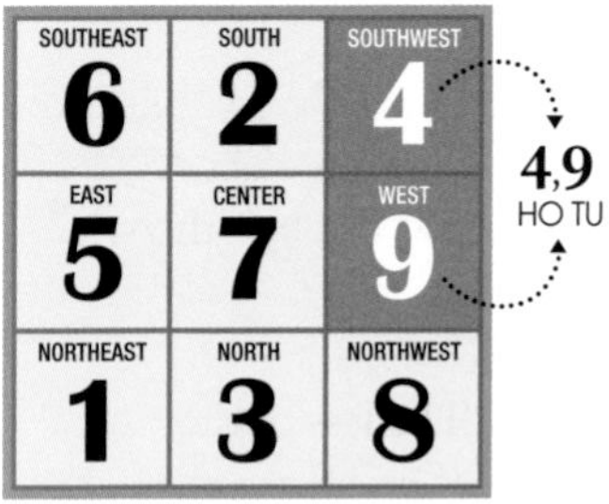

SOUTHEAST 6	SOUTH 2	SOUTHWEST 4
EAST 5	CENTER 7	WEST 9
NORTHEAST 1	NORTH 3	NORTHWEST 8

4,9
HO TU

When we look at the WEST sector, we see that there is the auspicious HO TU combination of 4/9 combining SW/ West. This Ho Tu brings prosperity and indicates better heads will prevail whenever anger energies threaten to erupt.

And in the sector of NW where the previous year's ferocious Dog resides, we see the benevolent and auspicious #8 star bringing lucky and auspicious energies. The #8 is also an Earth star and it is calming in its influence this year.

Note that it is the NW sector where the #8 resides, and because it brings clarity of thinking and good decision-making to this sector, the patriarchal leaders of the world are likely to benefit from this influence.

The #8 in the NW is an excellent placement indeed, manifesting good administrative capability in leaders of the world and good judgment in the patriarchal bosses within organizations and commercial corporations. More than likely then, 2020 will see growth and positive developments experienced by many people, bringing about new prosperity. This can override the unfriendly energies generated by the #7 star holding sway as the center star through the year.

A MORE STABLE YEAR

The good news is that there will be less of the upheavals of Earth and Water of previous years. In 2020, we see the sign of the Rat bringing a period of good energies that provides for sustained development. Its Water element brings stable power, and it nurtures Wood, which brings growth. There is respect for those exercising power, so law and order proceeds more smoothly in most countries.

GETTING STARTED

The main problem for many in 2020 is getting started. There are likely to be obstacles that cause delays. Problems arise that slow down the start of projects, and the transformation of ideas into action meet with hindrances. This is caused by the #7 star creating uncertainties.

THE PRESENCE OF LAP CHUN

However, the start of the lunar new year takes place on 25th January. This means there is the lap chun in 2020, which means that projects can get started smoothly. There is excellent spring luck for the year, so those wanting to initiate new undertakings can do so confident in the knowledge that this is a good year to pursue new directions. Growth is assured.

ACTIVATE THE LAP CHUN:

Carry this year's specially designed **Annual Amulet 2020** which features the ruling animal sign of the year the Rat on one side with Lotus and Flowers to signify growth, and with the Rat's astrological ally the mighty Dragon on the other side shown with Ru Yi and ingots for power and wealth.

This annual amulet symbolises you benefitting fully from the presence of the Lap Chun this year while staying protected against the worst of its afflictions.

MONEY TO BE MADE

The prospects for the global economy are promising. There will be sufficient resources and new wealth can get created. There is enough prosperity to make many people happy. There is money to be made. In fact, for those who are able to tap into personal veins of good fortune, 2020 can turn out to be a breakout year indeed.

This is a promise of the Rat Year, which is always a great year to create new wealth. The Rat is the sign that is famous for having the capability to eke out prosperity from very minimal resources.

Rat years are always years when money can be made! Display the Wealth Mongoose Spouting Jewels in the NW this year.

Unfortunately in 2020, the Rat sector of the NORTH plays host to the TAI SUI and it also faces the energy of the Three Killings. This double affliction directly facing the Rat's sector of North brings distractions and unfortunate obstacles – big and small. Many of these problems will arise from small-mindedness, manifesting as problems within interpersonal relationships. It causes people to get sidetracked and distracted. This is a year when it is a challenge to stay focused.

OUTLOOK FOR THE 12 ANIMALS

The **ROOSTER** enjoys the promise of great good fortune coming, brought by the stars of *Big Auspicious* in the 24 Mountains compass of 2020. How much of this good luck potential can materialize will depend on this sign's creativity and intelligence. But with the #9 star in its sector, there is excellent completion luck. The Rooster gets stronger this year and continues on from the previous year's fast pace of activities.

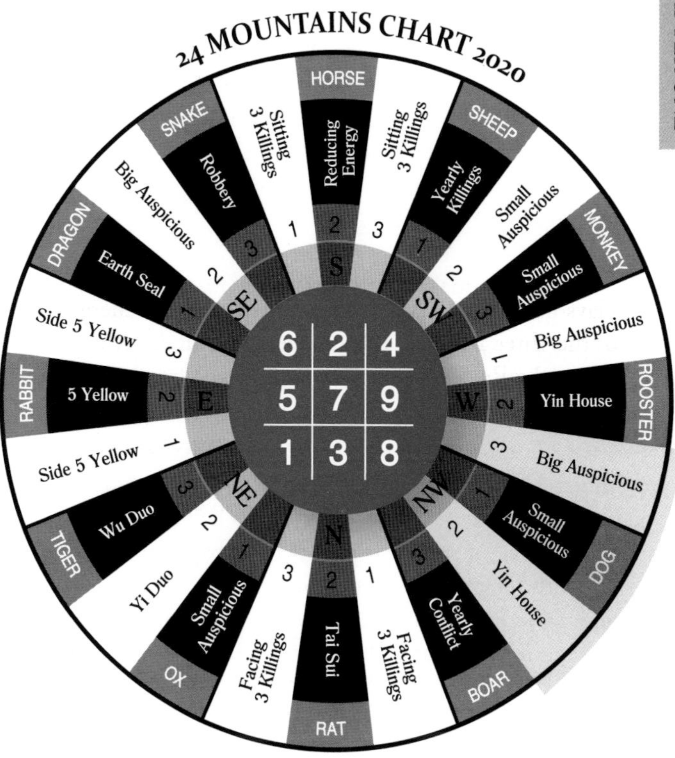

24 Mountains Compass of 2020
and its influence on the luck of the 12 animal signs.

But there is a *Star of Yin House* sitting in its sector and this suggests the possibility of there being the loss of someone close. Subdue bad vibes of this *Yin House Star* by displaying the **Yang Energy Amulet** in the West corner of the home. It is MOST important to suppress this affliction if there are old people living in the home.

Two other animal signs enjoying *Big Auspicious* are those born in the years of the **DRAGON** and **SNAKE**. For these two signs, heaven luck shines bright, so there are unexpected windfalls coming their way. It is a good idea to enhance with a **Heaven Luck Enhancing Mirror** for this incredible good luck to manifest. Carrying good luck charms that bring success such as **Windhorse hangings** is the way to go for this pair of signs this year. It is an excellent idea for both Dragon and Snake to energize the *Star of Big Auspicious* that lies between their sectors in the SE by placing the **Treasure Chest Dharani** in the SE of the home to attract good fortune energy.

The Dragon also enjoys the luck of the *Earth Seal,* which brings excellent grounding luck, but for the Snake, good fortune indications gets clouded by the danger of getting robbed this year. The Snake must make certain to carry the **Anti-Robbery Amulet** this year. The Dragon must carry or display the **Earth Seal Amulet** to ensure its intrinsic Earth element does not get diluted this year.

In 2020, the sign of the East is afflicted by the *Five Yellow* and hence requires the help of the **Five Element Pagoda**. The sign of the **RABBIT** must watch that the bad luck brought by this afflictive star does not bring mischief its way. The Rabbit definitely needs to display the Five Element Pagoda cure prominently in its sector to subdue all the bad luck vibrations brought by the *wu wang* star of #5. In 2020, the Rabbit should watch its back, as it is likely to suffer the consequences of some old grievance surfacing that could cause plenty of worry and trouble.

The **SHEEP** sits on the *Star of Yearly Killings*, a minor afflictive star, but its sector mate the **MONKEY** brings a double dose of auspicious energy from *Small Auspicious stars* that bring good energy in small doses through the year. The Sheep must subdue the "killing" energy and enhance the auspicious chi coming from the direction of the Monkey. The best way to do this is to place a **Bejewelled Reflecting Mirror** facing towards the Monkey and Rooster directions (i.e. the West).

The **MONKEY** in 2020 is on a roll and should have no problem staying ahead of the competition, especially those working in professional careers or competing for high honours of some kind. It sits on and is flanked by *Small and Big Auspicious* stars in 2020. Those doing business get assistance easily and those still at school will find the year bringing many small and big successes. This sign should however be careful not to get distracted by romantic inclinations. It benefits to stay cool and detached this year.

The **TIGER** will have a relatively quiet year, while the **OX** sits on a *Star of Small Auspicious*. This is a year of many small victories brought by the Victory Star 1 in their sector. This year, it is a good idea to place victory-enhancing and other **success symbols** in the NE sector. Using A*rt of Placement* feng shui benefits these two signs. Thus display the **Windhorse-Boosting Victory Flag** and the powerful **Red Windhorse** in the Northeast to attract success luck for both signs.

The **RAT** and **HORSE** should work at generating good energy and strengthening themselves in 2020. The Rat plays host to the *TAI SUI* who is the God of the Year (a very good thing), while the Horse sits on the *Star of Reducing Energy*. Both signs face their respective challenges in 2020 and are in need of help from powerful energizing Deities such as **Kuan Kung** or the **Four Heavenly Kings**.

Those who understand the role of symbolic placement power in feng shui know that the mere presence of these Taoist Deities radiate good fortune vibes wherever they are placed, but especially when there are afflictive stars present. It is for this reason that these Taoist deities have retained their huge popularity through the centuries. Even until today, you can see their images on many decorative display items in homes across China, and in Chinese homes all round the world.

The **BOAR** and **DOG** enjoy the magical sign of 8 in 2020. The Dog also has a *Small Auspicious Star* so that the year brings many small victories. The Boar however must contend with the *Yearly Conflict Star* and is well advised to refrain from getting into arguments with others. The Boar and Dog should display the **Wealth Tree with Mongoose** in the NW.

CHAPTER 2

FOUR PILLARS CHART 2020

FOUR PILLARS CHART 2020

HOUR	DAY	MONTH	YEAR
己 Yin Earth	丁 Yin Fire	戊 Yang Earth	庚 Yang Metal
辛 酉 Yin Metal Rooster	己 丑 Yin Earth Ox	甲 寅 Yang Wood Tiger	壬 子 Yang Water Rat

THE YEAR'S FOUR PILLARS

To get an overall feel for the destiny outlook of the year, we must analyze the year's Four Pillars chart. This reveals the impact of the five elements interacting with the animal signs in the year's chart. The various combinations within the chart offer insights into what's in store. Thus we take a look at the eight elements dominating the Four Pillars of the year's Paht Chee chart. We look at the way the heavenly stems and earthly branches combine together, and further examine the luck pillars of the 12 months of the year.

The 2020 Paht Chee chart reveals a year when all five elements are present. This indicates a well-balanced year where nothing is missing.

EARTH BRINGS CREATIVITY

There is dominance of EARTH energy, but the ruling element is weak YIN fire. This will be a harmonious year when good sense and logical minds exert a big influence, so there should not be any very major conflicts, and focus will be on the search for knowledge. 2020 is a year when a renewed respect rises for those with creativity and intelligence. It will be an extremely beneficial year for those seeking knowledge.

HOUR	DAY	MONTH	YEAR
己 Yin Earth	丁 Yin Fire	戊 Yang Earth	庚 Yang Metal
辛 酉 Yin Metal Rooster	己 丑 Yin Earth Ox	甲 寅 Yang Wood Tiger	壬 子 Yang Water Rat

The 2020 Paht Chee chart is dominated by **Earth**, which represents intelligence and creativity this year.

NO MISSING ELEMENTS

A quick glance at the Paht Chee chart reveals all five elements are present, implying there is no imbalance of energies. We also see that the YEAR Pillar has Metal PRODUCING Water, and in the DAY Pillar, Fire is PRODUCING Earth. These are the two most important pillars, and with the elements in a productive relationship, there is favourable indication of excellent productivity. There is hence a productive yin and a productive yang pillar in the chart.

	"Productive"		"Productive"
HOUR	**DAY**	**MONTH**	**YEAR**
己 Yin Earth	丁 Yin Fire	戊 Yang Earth	庚 Yang Metal
辛 酉 Yin Metal Rooster	己 丑 Yin Earth Ox	甲 寅 Yang Wood Tiger	壬 子 Yang Water Rat

The two most important pillars - the **Year Pillar** and the **Day Pillar** - are both in productive relationship, one being Yang in nature, the other Yin.

RELATIONSHIPS GET A BOOST

Rooster and Ox in the HOUR and DAY pillars are indication of good rapport between parents and children. Good sense prevails in the bringing up of children this year. Relationships between spouses are harmonious as indicated by the productive elements. Here, Fire produces Earth, indicating greater domestic harmony in 2020.

Rat and Ox in the YEAR and DAY pillars are further indication that despite the discordant #7 in the center of the year's Flying Star chart, relationships will stay resilient despite temporary difficulties.

HOUR	DAY	MONTH	YEAR
己 Yin Earth	丁 Yin Fire	戊 Yang Earth	庚 Yang Metal
辛 酉 Yin Metal **Rooster**	己 丑 Yin Earth **Ox**	甲 寅 Yang Wood Tiger	壬 子 Yang Water Rat

Allies (Rooster – Ox)

Secret Friend/Soulmate Combination (Ox – Rat)

The **Rooster** and **Ox** in the Hour and Day Plllars suggest excellent rapport between parents and children in 2020, while the **Rat** and **Ox** in the Year and Day Pillars point to long term bonds reigning supreme over short term conflicts.

Rat and Ox are secret friends and soulmates of the zodiac, and the presence of this combination in the Earthly branches suggest that while on the surface things may be challenging, good sense will ultimately prevail. Bridges do not get burned over petty, inconsequential matters.

> Rat Years are years when opportunities for enhancing family prosperity motivates the younger members of the family to think up wonderful new ideas..

It is advisable never to dismiss fresh ideas offered by the younger members of the family. The world is evolving, and increasingly, our "young ones" are bringing invaluable new perspectives to the way we live, work and enjoy life.

WEALTH LUCK BROUGHT BY METAL ELEMENT

The Metal Rat Year is a pacifying year filled with many prosperity opportunities. It benefits to view the year positively, as the coming twelve months from February 4th 2020 till February 4th 2021 will see many fresh new opportunities for creating wealth. It is beneficial to live in a state of awareness, being totally mindful to new

avenues for growth and development. This is a year when being creative reaps dividends.

There is wealth luck available to be tapped. What is needed is a keen eye and the motivation to get started and to take action. Think outside the box and look for new ways of producing, packaging and marketing goods and services.

The global business scenario has been changing fast in the past decade. Breakthrough technology and applications bring many prominent players into the technology game. The good news is that anyone can take fullest advantage of the global scenario for commerce to flourish in the digital and internet age.

We have been living in the Period of 8 which has favoured China, but the Period of 9 is coming, and it is a great idea for anyone looking to the longer term future and keen on building their businesses to start looking SOUTH, as this is the coming of the Period of 9 and energy strength is pointing us to this direction for new expansion and growth chances.

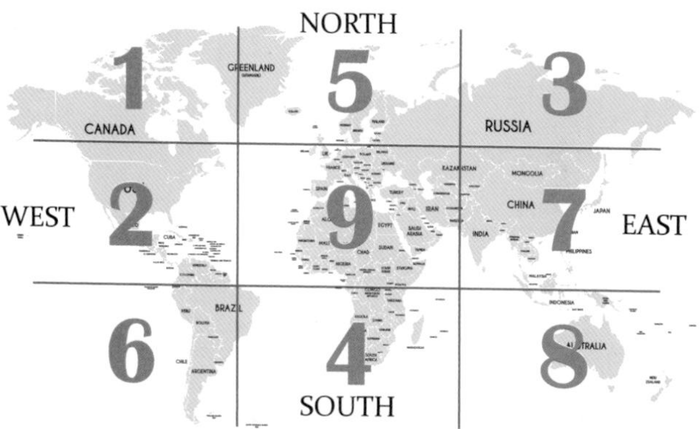

As we enter the last quarter of Period 8 and approach the Period of 9, global growth opportunities are likely to change.

HIDDEN STARS OF 2020

A very positive aspect of the coming year is the appearance of three very lucky stars - the *Star of Scholastic Brilliance*, the *Commanding Star* and the *Star of Powerful Mentors*. These are hidden stars brought by the year's Paht Chee chart, and what they suggest is the potential for new inventions, new innovations and exciting new directions in business and commerce, and in one's personal endeavours.

STAR OF SCHOLASTIC BRILLIANCE

COMMANDING STAR

STAR OF POWERFUL MENTORS

On a macro level, the world will likely see a further shift to an even more digitalized age, led by the brilliant young minds of tomorrow. On a personal level, all three special stars indicate the presence of superior intellect, superior mentors and guidance, and the self-motivation to pursue excellence in whatever one may be engaged in. There is likely to be unprecedented innovation and originality of thought, advancing our existence in multiple directions. There will continue to be huge leaps and advances in the way we work, the way we play and the way we live.

Money will no longer be made through conventional means. Those who make it big will be those who can spot windows of opportunity and who then go after these opportunities with speed and gusto.

ACTIVATION IS NEEDED!

The most important thing to remember when you read this book is that in Chinese destiny analysis, we do not hold the Western view that one's destiny is set in stone. Indeed, the Four Pillars chart is not a "prediction" as such, it is a road map to success which can be followed to benefit from the myriad opportunities presented by the year.

> To the Chinese, for good fortune to manifest, one has to infuse each one of these indications with *yang* energy. One has to breathe *life* into them.

The lucky indications of the year must be activated for their effects to be felt. This should be done both with self-effort as well as the placement of the correct symbols and enhancers, if one is to enjoy its benefits to the fullest.

1 *STAR OF SCHOLASTIC BRILLIANCE* *enhances the power of scholarship*

This star makes an appearance again in this year's chart, indicating that scholarship and academic excellence continues to open doors to the best jobs and the best opportunities. Those with scholastic honours and accolades to their names continue to impress and the benefits of their qualifications go beyond the knowledge and skills acquired during their courses of study.

The *Scholastic Brilliance Star* of 2020 gets formed by the year's self element of YIN FIRE with the ROOSTER in the Hour Pillar.

HOUR	DAY	MONTH	YEAR
己 Yin Earth	丁 Yin Fire	戊 Yang Earth	庚 Yang Metal
辛 酉 Yin Metal Rooster	己 丑 Yin Earth Ox	甲 寅 Yang Wood Tiger	壬 子 Yang Water Rat

The Star of Scholastic Brilliance brings success to those pursuing knowledge & scholastic endeavours.

Of all the twelve signs, the Rooster is the most akin to paying meticulous attention to detail. Together with its natural flair for pomp and paegentry, this indicates that success in academic endeavours will come to those who combine resilient hard work with the ability to demonstrate that work at the right time.

The Yin Fire indicates that it will be those capable of short sharp spurts of brilliance who will get noticed rather than the solid workhorse who ploughs through slow and steady. This is not to say that consistent good work is unimportant, only that this year, those who rise to the fore to shine will be those who make it a part of their plan to shine at the right time.

Fire is an element that is bright and brilliant, but it is also an element that requires fuel to sustain it. Similarly, to achieve scholastic brilliance this year will require the continued drive and motivation to succeed, coupled with attention to detail when it counts the most - exam time. That it is Yin Fire (rather than Yang) re-emphasizes the need for the stamina to stay the course, simmering and smoldering with periods of brilliant fire.

To activate this year's *Scholastic Brilliance Star*, we suggest the **13-level Bejewelled Wisdom Pagoda** in bright red. This pagoda not only epitomizes examination and scholastic success for children, it also empowers the young adult looking to make a name for him or herself in the working world.

Containing the most precious *Treasure Chest Dharani* sutra, placed on the workdesk, it empowers you with countless blessings to excel in all your endeavours. You can also place it in the SW which houses the Scholastic Star of the year, or the West, which is flanked by two stars of Big Auspicious.

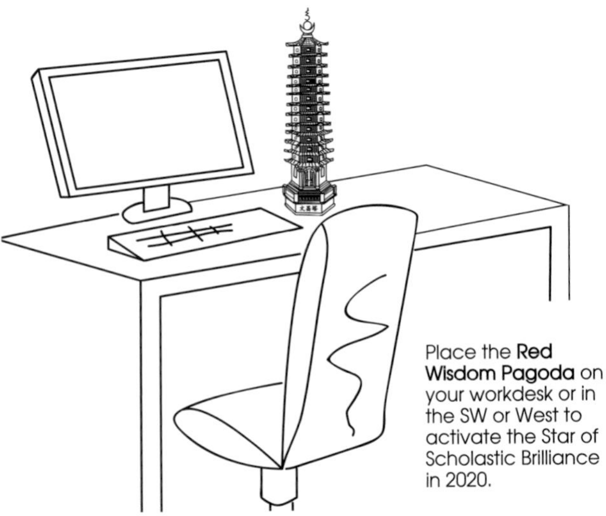

Place the **Red Wisdom Pagoda** on your workdesk or in the SW or West to activate the Star of Scholastic Brilliance in 2020.

2 *COMMANDING STAR brings benevolent leaders*

The outstandingly auspicious Commanding Star is formed by the combination of the OX in the Day Pillar with the ROOSTER in the Hour Pillar.

This set of allies from the Trinity of Intellectuals suggests that power and influence lies with superior mindpower. It will be intellect that is admired and revered, and that will provide leaders with what they need to lead. Leaders, bosses and anyone in a position of command will find it far more effective to lead with brains than with brawn this year.

HOUR	DAY	MONTH	YEAR
己 Yin Earth	丁 Yin Fire	戊 Yang Earth	庚 Yang Metal
辛 酉 Yin Metal Rooster	己 丑 Yin Earth Ox	甲 寅 Yang Wood Tiger	壬 子 Yang Water Rat

The **Commanding Star** brings authority and influence, benefitting those in positions of authority.

The appearance of this star together with the powerful #8 in the NW, the sector of the leader, suggests 2020 will bring wise and benevolent leadership at all levels.

> The Commanding Star brings authority, power and influence luck to the year, benefitting those who find themselves in positions of authority.

Indeed the year benefits those who know how to use their influence and power, so managers with a clear idea of their strategy or focus will benefit especially from this star. Leaders will find the energy of the year increases their effectiveness, and the mantle of leadership comes easily for them.

FENG SHUI ENHANCER: To activate the luck of the Commanding Star, display the **Jade Emperor Heaven Amulet** in a prominent place in the Northwest of your home or living room, or on your office or study desk where you work.

If you hold a CEO, managerial or leadership position at work, you should also have the **Three Warriors - Zhang Fei, Kuan Kung and Liu Bei** in your office. These are the three great heroes of Chinese history, who personify courage, integrity and honour. They symbolize success achieved through clever strategy and effective diplomacy; beating the competition without having to resort to undesirable or underhanded tactics.

Anyone in a position of leadership should have the Three Warriors Liu Bei, Kuan Kung and Zhang Fei in the office. They bring forth the Commanding Star of the year for effective leadership and powerful influence.

3 *STAR OF POWERFUL MENTORS* *brings support of influential people*

This star is brought by the OX in the Day Pillar and the Heavenly Stem of YANG METAL in the Year Pillar. This year's *Star of Powerful Mentors* suggests that for the younger generation determined to succeed, the year will be filled with influential people turning up in their lives to give them strong, meaningful and powerful support.

HOUR	DAY	MONTH	YEAR
己 Yin Earth	丁 Yin Fire	戊 Yang Earth	庚 Yang Metal
辛 酉 Yin Metal Rooster	己 丑 Yin Earth Ox	甲 寅 Yang Wood Tiger	壬 子 Yang Water Rat

The **Star of Powerful Mentors** brings support from influential people.

The presence of this star is a reminder to heed the advice of those in the generation above you. Although much of the action this year will involve the youth and younger generation, the older folk will have plenty of influence in the background.

The animal signs that stand to gain most from the *Star of Powerful Mentors* in 2020 are the **Dragon, Snake, Rooster** and **Rat**.

These signs, and all other signs, should activate this star by displaying the **9-Dragon Kuan Kung** facing the front door of the home. You can also display Kuan Kung behind you at your desk for support from important people in a position to help you.

Display the 9-Dragon Kuan Kung in the vicinity of your main door to activate Star of Powerful Mentors.

IMPORTANCE OF A STRONG LIFE FORCE

Whatever a year holds in store, to benefit fully from the auspicious indications on offer, one has to have sufficient Life Force. This year, those benefitting from excellent levels of Life Force continue to be the WOOD signs of **Tiger** and **Rabbit,** while the EARTH signs of **Ox, Dragon, Sheep** and **Dog** continue to enjoy very good levels. For these six signs, you are blessed with the ability to turn ideas into reality. You are constantly filled with an inner drive, which keeps you resolute and very action-oriented. You enjoy a strong self-conviction and will not be easily flustered or swayed.

The Earth signs of Ox, Dragon, Sheep and Dog and Wood signs of Tiger and Rabbit enjoy excellent levels of Life Force, allowing them to make the most of the opportunities brought by the 2020 chart.

The WATER signs of **Rat** and **Boar** have good levels of Life Force, while the METAL signs of **Monkey** and **Rooster** have neutral levels.

The FIRE signs of **Snake** and **Horse** continue to suffer from very poor levels of Life Force. Both Snake and Horse thus MUST make every effort to increase their personal Life Force levels or they could find themselves succumbing to defeat before they even get started.

FENG SHUI CURE: Carry the **Life Force Enhancing Amulet** at all times, and constantly work at building up your own self-confidence and self-esteem.

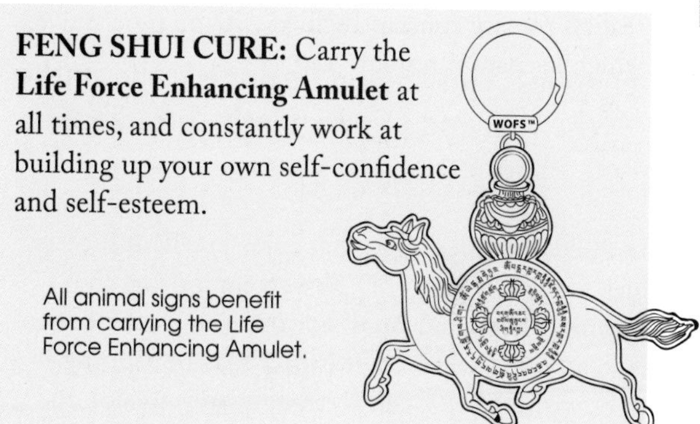

All animal signs benefit from carrying the Life Force Enhancing Amulet.

Both Snake and Horse need to be especially watchful of the company they keep. Surrounding oneself with "friends" who make you feel inferior or inadequate is the surest way of ensuring you fail to overcome the year's afflictions.

STRENGTHENING SUCCESS LUCK in 2020

While all the ingredients are there for the coming Rat Year to be good one, this can only be done with sufficient *Lung Ta* levels. When your personal *lung ta* or Windhorse is weak, no matter how hard you try or what strings you manage to pull, success will prove elusive.

What everyone should do as a matter of course each year is to raise their Windhorse energies. This should be done at the start of the year and also regularly throughout the year.

In 2020, the three signs that enjoy excellent success luck are the *Trinity of Diplomats* comprising the **Rabbit, Sheep** and **Boar**. For these signs, the advice is to go for it, whatever it is they may be aspiring to or wishing for. Luck is strongly on your side and everything you put your focus on succeeds easily, with results coming quickly. The *Trinity of Adventurers* made up of **Dog, Horse** and **Tiger** also have good levels of *lung ta* in 2020. These signs too can proceed with confidence in whatever they set their minds to.

But the *Trinity of Intellectuals* comprising **Snake, Rooster** and **Ox**, and the *Trinity of Competitors* made up of **Rat, Dragon** and **Monkey** have neutral and bad levels of *lung ta* respectively, so for them, we strongly suggest carrying **Windhorse amulets** to boost their potential for success.

The best way to boost one's success luck for the year is to carry the Windhorse as a portable amulet and display a prominent Windhorse within sight of your workdesk.

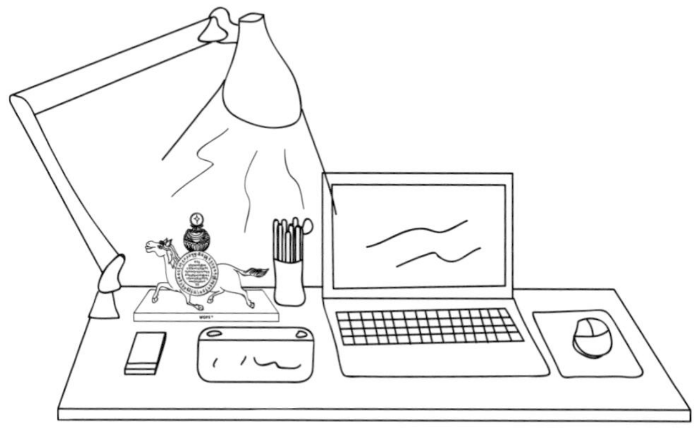

Boost success luck with the Windhorse. Display on your desk for your endeavours to go smoothly. It helps ensure you can overcome whatever obstacles may crop up, and meet with success in all that you do.

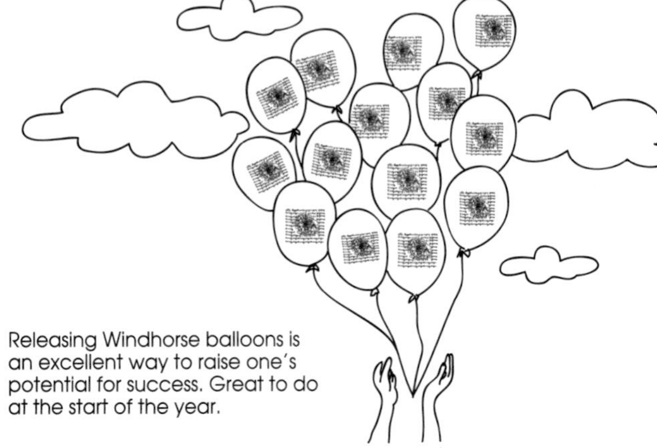

Releasing Windhorse balloons is an excellent way to raise one's potential for success. Great to do at the start of the year.

It is also incredibly effective to regularly perform Windhorse balloon rituals (we print the Windhorse mantras on five-element coloured balloons and these are made available for purchase on *www.fsmegamall.com* for those who would like to perform this ritual.)

Once a month - or more regularly if you like - fill Windhorse balloons with helium and display them for at least one full day. Make sure you have one balloon in each of the five colours of RED, WHITE, BLUE, YELLOW and GREEN as you recite the Windhorse mantra while making a heartfelt wish.

The Windhorse Mantra:
KI KI SO SO LAJA LO

CHAPTER

3

LUCK OF THE DOG IN 2020

A year for Dog to expand your horizons

ELEMENT LUCK OF THE

DOG 2020	YEAR ELEMENT	FIRE DOG *74/14 Years*	EARTH DOG *62 Years*
LIFE FORCE	**WATER**	Very Good OO	Very Good OO
HEALTH	**EARTH**	Good O	Very Good OO
WEALTH	**METAL**	Very Good OO	Neutral OX
SUCCESS (*Lung Ta*)	**WOOD**	Very Good OO	Very Good OO
SPIRIT ESSENCE	**METAL**	Very Good OO	Very Good OO

DOG 2020

METAL DOG *50 Years*	WATER DOG *38 Years*	WOOD DOG *86/26 Years*
Very Good OO	Very Good OO	Very Good OO
Excellent OOO 👍	Very Bad XX	Neutral OX
Bad X	Excellent OOO 👍	Very Bad XX
Very Good OO	Very Good OO	Very Good OO
Very Good OO	Very Good OO	Very Good OO

ELEMENT LUCK OF THE DOG IN 2020

The chart in the previous spread summarizes how the Dog's personal elements interact with those of the year 2020 in five important luck categories. An important category is the one that denotes success luck for the year, and everyone born under the sign of Dog enjoys very good success luck. This indicates that the Dog's chances of achieving success in 2020 are very good indeed.

The Dog's life force and spirit essence are also at very good levels. This indicates that those belonging to this sign are likely to benefit from being very resilient, possessing strong determination through the year. You start the year very confident, and you approach new responsibilities placed on your willing shoulders with confidence.

In 2020, the Dog has self-assurance written all over its smiling face. You approach work-related matters in a manner that reflects your inner attitude, with impressive spirit showing through in whatever projects you take on. You exude an enormous poise in the way you approach every new responsibility, even to the extent of sometimes coming across arrogant and conceited.

The Dog is going through a popular time and many view you in a very positive light. Your attitude is upbeat and this helps you come across as a winner in everything you do, so others forgive your touch of superciliousness, as long as it stays just a touch. This sign is on a roll and no matter what you take on, luck is on your side!

This is a year when everything you touch turns to gold. At work, you impress boss and underlings alike, with the secure way in which you approach every task. Your sense of confidence is infectious, and in this way you make a good leader, sharing your assurance with those who follow you in a very positive way. Your peers are likely to lean quite heavily on you this year. They take confidence from the self-assurance you exude.

Success breeds success, as a result of which your success luck is shared by those around you. Your self-assuredness is more than justified because you possess noticeable strength in the actions you initiate. This year then, you will be hard to beat. But understand that others who watch your easy success can consciously or sub-consciously direct arrows of jealousy your way. Do not feel discouraged; instead, work on winning them over!

> The good thing about 2020 is that your luck is strong so you are not easily distracted. You possess a steely-eyed determination in everything you take on.

Remember, you are the Dog, one of the trinity of very strong signs that include the Tiger and Horse, so you have speed and courage as secondary attributes. You are alert to warning signs, thus whatever negative energies blow your way are met with a state of readiness. Being alert to warning signals comes naturally to your sign.

You are also keen to demonstrate your reliability. You like it when others depend on you. As a result, you inspire others with your expectations of positive outcomes. In 2020, you go through a good year, so work goals benefit from an impressive clarity of intention. There is admirable conscious awareness of your own abilities. This helps you take on strong leadership roles this year. Those of you called upon to lead should accept without hesitation.

Your element luck chart looks extremely supportive of all your efforts. As a result, you are perfectly poised to make the most of the powerful #8 star which brings auspicious winds your way. The energies of the year are extremely supportive of your sign.

All your efforts are likely to bear fruit and the year will end on a very good note for you. The Dog's element luck in 2020 is sustained by very good life force and spirit essence, indications that give you strength and confidence to perform at your very best. Whatever you do this year, the energies that blow your way are supportive and upbeat.

Those with specific tasks at hand can take heart that you will not lose the momentum needed to see through your particular assignments. Should you face moments of uncertainty, the advice is to persevere regardless, and the success you have been expecting will be yours.

In 2020, the young **26 year old Wood Dog** and the older **50 year old Metal Dog** may suffer some financial setback, but this is unlikely to be serious. Nevertheless, you must not allow such obstacles make you doubt yourself. This is a very good year for the Dog and ultimately, even if there are glitches through the year, they will not be serious. The ultimate result by year end is extremely positive. Mostly, this Year of the Rat is a time when you are likely to see auspicious energies bringing good news for you.

Your element luck suggests you can expect many of your aspirations to work out very well. Success manifests in a clear and obvious manner, so 2020 is likely to be satisfying and gratifying. Remember this whenever self-doubt causes you to feel uncertain.

Those doing business enjoy positive developments, and those working their way up the career ladder meet with opportunities for upward mobility. The **38 year old Water Dog** enjoys excellent wealth luck, while the **50 year old Metal Dog** has excellent health indications. All those belonging to the Dog sign irrespective of your heavenly stem benefit from very good *lung ta,* which brings ready success. The Dog in 2020 should boost good fortune by displaying the **Windhorse-Boosting Victory Flag** in the NW. This should activate the good fortune winds of the year and bring five element power to everything you take on.

To strengthen success further, place the **Red Windhorse** in front of you on your work desk. This powerful symbol always strengthens success energy around you. It attracts invisible support from the cosmic warrior King Gesar, bringing attainment luck to all who send out invisible signals to this wonderful warrior king.

The other thing you can do to improve your success essence is to increase the presence of EARTH element energy. Place a *Citrine Tree* in the NW.

Your citrine tree can be as large as you wish, but its size should complement the size of your home, or of the room in which you display the tree. Remember that for your sign, Earth is also excellent for activating wealth luck. When the Earth element of your sign strengthens the Metal element of the NW, for 2020 it will also strengthen your personal prospects for wealth.

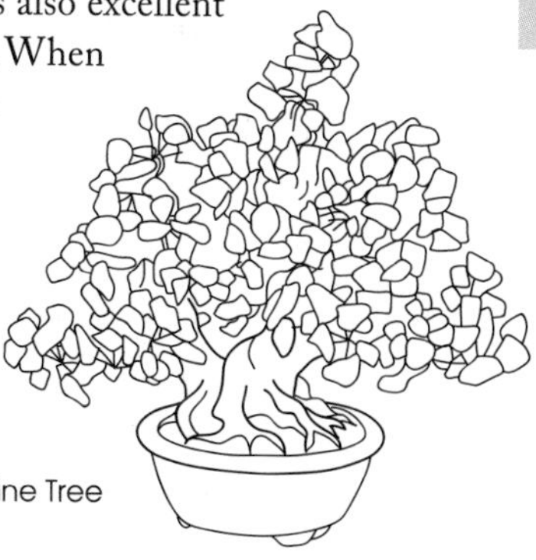

Citrine Tree

This is a good year to broaden your outlook and to expand your reach. Any kind of expansion brings long-term benefits to the Dog this year. Do not hesitate to work on ideas or to call on help should you need it. You work well with others and you have the kind of energy that inspires others this year.

The Dog is most defintiely in a good place. It is a very beneficial year to place images of **your own symbolic sign** in the NW sector. Collect **Dog figurines** and empower your own animal sign luck by displaying them in the home. Different breeds evoke different qualities; pick dog breeds that symbolise auspicious attributes to you. For example, the Golden Retriever denotes loyalty, bringing loyal friends your way. The Border Collie denotes intelligence. The Poodle symbolises class and elegance. The Yorkshire Terrier denotes companionship. The Afghan Hound suggests nobility.

Those born under the sign of Dog benefit from placing images of your own sign within the home.

These are general universal attributes assigned to these breeds, but you should fill your home with dogs that connect psychically with you on some level, and that suggest the kind of qualities you would like to see in yourself and in the people who make up your life.

FIRE DOG 26 Years	
LIFE FORCE	VERY GOOD
HEALTH	NEUTRAL
WEALTH	VERY BAD
SUCCESS *(Lung Ta)*	VERY GOOD
SPIRIT ESSENCE	VERY GOOD

The **26 YEAR OLD FIRE DOG** should focus on building resources for the future. This is not a year to take financial risks or for pursuing get-rich-quick schemes. Your wealth luck is weak so it does not support taking monetary risks. You are better off staying on the conservative side when it comes to financial matters, and to focus on other dimensions of attainment open to you.

With wealth luck at a low level, you must exercise caution when investing. Indeed, this is not a good year to put yourself on the line. By all means go ahead and seek excitement, but focus on areas that do not involve putting your money at risk. You are lucky this year, as other dimensions of your element luck are looking good; but this is a year to divert attention to doing things that motivate you. Take joy and satisfaction not just from the monetary aspects of an endeavour. Be encouraged knowing that you enjoy success luck. If you're looking for financial success, it will come with time, though don't expect a huge bonanza this year.

Your *lung ta* is very strong. Put focus on going after tangible goals that you may have previously put on hold. Be confident - this is a good year to pursue secret dreams. Do not fear failure. Harness the courage to strike out in directions that excite you.

Think positive about pursuing things that are untried. Following the road less travelled is exactly in sync with the Dog personality. If you shift your mindset towards exploration and discovery, you will likely find this year stimulating and fulfilling, setting you up for quite phenomenal success later on. Think of this as the kind of year where you lay the groundwork.

While the Dog sign may not be ostentatious or obvious, you are a brave sign, and your energy levels are high, making this a good time to go after directions that have always fascinated you. Your life force and spirit essence are at very good levels, and this suggests you have the vitality to be as adventurous as you wish. You can indulge yourself and follow your instincts, but be clever and calculate the probabilities whenever you take a gamble. Accept that you are young, so while you can afford to be adventurous, also refrain from being reckless.

WEALTH LUCK NEEDS SOME HELP: The **26 year old Dog** enjoys very good luck all round, just your wealth indications are less than stellar. Get yourself a **Wealth Cabinet** and display in front of you on your work desk, or on your vanity table.

Happiness and fulfilment for this Dog will come from personal achievements that need not be linked to how much money you make or have. Strengthen your success luck which is already at a very good level by wearing the **Windhorse in 22K gold plate**.

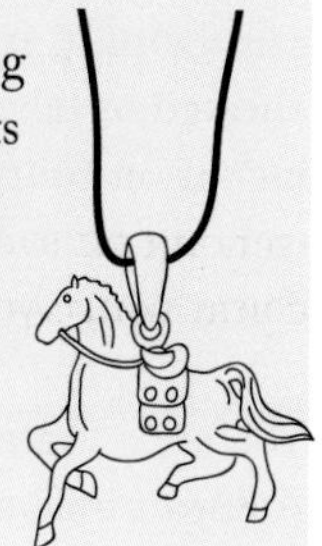

WATER DOG 38 Years	
LIFE FORCE	VERY GOOD
HEALTH	VERY BAD
WEALTH	EXCELLENT
SUCCESS *(Lung Ta)*	VERY GOOD
SPIRIT ESSENCE	VERY GOOD

The **38 YEAR OLD WATER DOG** is very lucky in its wealth category, so you can be as courageous as you wish when it comes to financial matters. You possess the best combination possible in this category, so you are safe being open in the way you approach investments and also in the way you do business.

You can expand or diversify into new areas, and you can afford to trust others more, without fear of being cheated or taken advantage of. Whatever your strategy, luck is on your side. Whatever you undertake is likely to bring plum financial rewards, and others can even come along for the ride.

You are a Water Dog, and this year, the Water of the ruling animal sign of Rat syncs fabulously with your heavenly stem. Carry the **Mongoose Wealth Amulet** to strengthen wealth luck in everything you do. Be vigorous in formulating new directions for growth and expansion. Those pursuing career success can also be hard lined when investigating new possibilities.

Indeed, when wealth luck is indicating its best level for you, it is the time to actively seek out new opportunities.

Be open to proposals that come your way. Being lucky means opportunities find their way to you, but to benefit from them, you still need to make a judgement call on which ones to pursue. When you decide what to put your focus on, put your whole heart into it.

Your element luck in health however looks weak, so you need to be mindful of the pace at which you operate. Do not work yourself too hard or worry to an extent that your health gets compromised. At this age, you may tend to stress your physical capabilities, working non-stop without sufficient rest or recreation. You are at the prime of your life when your head is brimming with ideas – often to an extent that the physical body cannot keep up. Be mindful of this tendency, because this year, your health looks a little chancy. If you find yourself with insufficient sleep during the week days, make up for lost sleep during the weekends. The most important thing to remember is to get enough rest; this way you are making a specific effort to stay healthy. As long as you stay aware of this, you can keep yourself from descending into a downward spiral of malady which could take a long time to recover from.

LOOK AFTER YOUR HEALTH: Excellent luck all round for the **38 year old Dog**, with only your health indications looking problematic. Carry the **Wu Lou Garuda Health Amulet** and **Blue Mantra Wand** to counter your poor levels of health luck. While you are young and virile and strong, you are not invincible to falling sick. Take enough time out to rest if you feel yourself burning out, because if you fall sick, it could take a long time to recover, and if you burn out, restoring your emotional motivation will be even harder.

You are on a roll financially and one big success could boost your appetite for risk. Display the **Wealth Bull** on your desk to ensure wealth luck stays on your side through the year and have a **Wealth Cabinet** within view, which will help you amass asset wealth.

METAL DOG 50 Years	
LIFE FORCE	VERY GOOD
HEALTH	EXCELLENT
WEALTH	BAD
SUCCESS *(Lung Ta)*	VERY GOOD
SPIRIT ESSENCE	VERY GOOD

The **50 YEAR OLD METAL DOG** has its luck across the spectrum at very good levels, except in the area of wealth, which indicates a weak element combination. There is danger of money loss, so it is a year to refrain from taking big financial risks or from gambling too much. Those actively playing the stock markets should be careful of being overly aggressive with your strategies. If you can successfully take your mind off finance and business matters, and instead focus on enjoying the simpler things in life, this year suits you well indeed.

Health luck is at very good levels, which means you have wonderful vitality. You are in fine shape to lead an active and meaningful life.

A great year to travel, see the world and engage in activities you have always wanted to indulge in. But it is also a year when you can pursue work-related expansion or diversifications. As long as you stay within tested boundaries when it comes to taking risks, this is a year when you have the motivation to extend your reach. And because you enjoy very good success luck, your powerful *lung ta* spurs you onto ever higher levels of attainment.

You can be as confident as you wish, as your spirit essence supports your ambitious inclinations. You also have the life force to investigate new areas of expertise. With the digital age where it is, those extending your capabilities are sure to benefit.

Since health luck is looking good, you have the stamina and vitality to pursue new frontiers in your work. Do not be discouraged by your low levels of wealth luck, as profit rarely comes instantly. You should look on this as a year of new beginnings. Let yourself be inspired by your positive success luck indications. Push your own boundaries!

MONEY MATTERS: The **50 year old Dog** faces an extremely happy and satisfying year; the only source of worry is when it comes to money matters. You could lose money so it is best not to speculate or go out on a limb when it comes to big investment outlays. Preserve cash. Display the **Blue Wealth Cabinet** within easy view. This creates the energies that help to preserve your fortune.

EARTH DOG 62 Years	
LIFE FORCE	VERY GOOD
HEALTH	VERY GOOD
WEALTH	NEUTRAL
SUCCESS *(Lung Ta)*	VERY GOOD
SPIRIT ESSENCE	VERY GOOD

The **62 YEAR OLD EARTH DOG** enjoys very good element combinations in all its categories of luck except for the WEALTH category, which is at a neutral level. Your element chart shows you can take life easy, indulge in doing the things you enjoy, and forget about making money for a while. Spend time exploring the world and extending your interests beyond business and finance. It is not necessarily a year to think of "building". Instead, it is a year when you can "enjoy" the fruits of your many years of labour.

Learn to enjoy a life well-lived and pursue interests that may not offer so much in terms of financial gain. If you can ignore the money side of whatever interests you, or not put so much weight on it, doing things that take on fresh perspectives bring unexpected pleasure. And eventually, this can lead to financial gain as well.

In a year when we are entering a new calendar cycle, look on the bright side of whatever happens – a new grandchild, a new development in your company, a happy event within your family...

The key to having a great year is staying positive and adopting an optimistic outlook. Your sign is enjoying very good element luck, suggesting you can take the high road no matter what happens, especially in terms of interactions with relatives, and with respect to your relationship with your children and grandchildren.

Stay aloof from talking about money. Instead, focus on being chummy. At this age when you have already experienced so much of life, you can be magnanimous. Refrain from being judgmental or giving your opinion on personal matters if they are not all positive. Let the younger generation do their own thing, because like it or not, they really are different.

FOCUS ON YOUR SPIRITUALITY: This year the **62 year old Dog** should not place so much weight on financial matters. Learn to enjoy the simpler pleasures in life. Get yourself the **White Mantra Wand** and invoke the blessings of Vajrasattva, who purifies all negatives from your life leaving only happiness and harmony.

FIRE DOG 74 Years	
LIFE FORCE	VERY GOOD
HEALTH	GOOD
WEALTH	VERY GOOD
SUCCESS *(Lung Ta)*	VERY GOOD
SPIRIT ESSENCE	VERY GOOD

The **74 YEAR OLD FIRE DOG** has a very good year in all luck categories. There is nothing to worry about or to cause you concern. This year you can choose to live by any kind of lifestyle you wish - stay home, travel, become more active in charity work, or continue to advise for your own business.

In today's world, people are living longer and older folk continue to be mentally agile still. The Dog sign is especially alert this year, and those engaged in organizing events are likely to benefit the most. Diversity of experiences is what inspires you, and socializing with a wide spectrum of individuals brings the most enormous enjoyment.

The Dog sign always needs to be actively "doing something". At your age, engaging in helping others will tend to be the most fulfilling. You cannot stay at home watching TV or wasting away. The busier you are, the younger you stay.

Unless you have a "project" or "event" that engages you, you will not be able to assuage the restlessness within you. The busier you keep yourself, the happier you will be. Those who do not have an outlet for these restless feelings should seek out some activity that allows you to get moving!

WHITE TARA: For the **74 year old Dog,** you benefit from receiving blessings from White Tara, the Goddess of Longevity and Good Health. Carry the **White Tara Gau Home Amulet** and let her breathe renewed vigour into your being.

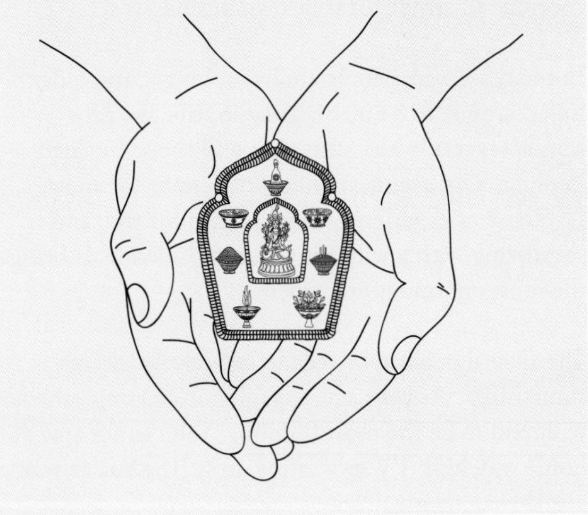

CHAPTER

4

FLYING STAR CHART OF 2020

FLYING STAR CHART OF 2020

Energies of loss & betrayal need to be subdued

The feng shui chart of the year which lays out the location of the year's flying stars in 2020 is dominated by the energy of 7, a troublesome star which can bring problems; it is the reigning number of this year's chart and its effectsmust be respected. More importantly, in any household, its energies must be subdued.

The 2020 chart is dominated by the violent star 7, which gets exacerbated by the 3 in the home sector of the animal sign of the year, the Rat.

CHAPTER FOUR

The number 7 is a Metal number that represents the negative side of relationships, symbolizing treachery, loss and betrayal.

More importantly, the number is strengthened by the Earth energy of the center grid, so the negative energies it releases - that of hostility that leads to quarrels - must be kept well under control.

Unfortunately, this year's animal sign of the Rat brings the Quarrelsome Star #3 into play. Here the number is located in the NORTH and because it is dominant this year, the #3 star aggravates the discordant vibrations of the year. This can cause the year's overriding energies to be rather hostile and suspicious.

Thus in spite of there being a good balance of elements in the year's Paht Chee, 2020 will nevertheless see a tendency towards confrontation. There is likely to be continued violence, both on the world stage as well as within countries and within household and individual situations.

It is thus judicious to always be careful and to play safe rather than be sorry. Treat the #7 star in the center with respect and actively subdue with feng shui cures and element antidotes.

This is a year when trickery and scheming are likely to occur more frequently than usual. This is brought about by a higher occurrence of betrayals and by the unbridled aggressiveness of ambitious people.

2020 is a year when the CENTER of buildings, houses and offices benefit from the presence of Water to subdue the strength of the 7.

Luckily, the 7 is a weak star in the current Period of 8, so it is easier to subdue. We are nevertheless nearing the end of Period of 8, with just 4 years remaining, so we need to keep in mind that the number 7 is re-strengthening. It is getting stronger even as we get nearer to Period 9.

Anything of a **black or dark blue colour** can work well at keeping the #7 under control. But it is advisable to make a concerted effort to do so in all homes and offices. This protects residents from becoming victims of unfair politicking and guard against troublemakers at the workplace.

In 2020, activate the **power of Water** in the home. Invest in a **small water feature** to create the presence of moving water in the CENTER grid of the home. You should also place the **Blue Rhino and Elephant with the Anti-Burglary Talisman** to suppress the negative influence of 7.

The luck of the different sectors of any abode is influenced by new energy brought by the year's feng shui chart. This chart reveals the year's auspicious

LO SHU SQUARE

SOUTHEAST	SOUTH	SOUTHWEST
4	9	2
EAST	CENTER	WEST
3	5	7
NORTHEAST	NORTH	NORTHWEST
8	1	6

FLYING STAR CHART OF 2020

SOUTHEAST	SOUTH	SOUTHWEST
6	2	4
EAST	CENTER	WEST
5	7	9
NORTHEAST	NORTH	NORTHWEST
1	3	8

On the left is the original Lo Shu chart. The right shows 2020's chart. At the start of each year, one of the most important things you must do is to take note of the new annual placement of the stars, and enhance and remedy each sector as needed.

and inauspicious sectors for all buildings, houses and apartments, and for individual rooms within buildings and homes.

The chart for 2020 reveals the different numbers in each of the nine grids in this 3x3 sector chart. This looks like the original Lo Shu square which reveals the role of numbers in time dimension feng shui. In each year, the numbers placed in each grid change according to the center number. With 7 in the center, the other numbers in the other eight sectors of the chart are then placed around the grid sectors. The sequence of placing the numbers follow the original Lo Shu flying star pattern and with each number bringing different kinds of luck to the different compass sectors; the luck of the different sectors can be analyzed and dealt with. This is what updating the feng shui of homes or office buildings means. Doing so correctly ensures good feng shui for the next twelve months.

The numbers that "fly" into each sector brings significanttransformations to the "luck outlook" not just of rooms located in the sectors; they also affect the luck of each of the animal signs, arising from the fact that each of the 12 signs occupies a particular compass sector influenced by each number.

The DOG person occupies the Northwest 1 location and enjoys the auspicious Prosperity Star of 8. There is thus a lot of wealth luck indicated for those born under the sign of Dog. The year holds out opportunities to augment your income streams, as well as to go after bigger wealth. With the *Big and Small Auspicious* luck brought to you by the 24 Mountains, this indicates that not only will you feel financially comfortable and secure this year, there will be new opportunities to raise your standard of living and to come into a windfall.

The Dog can invest and venture forth with confidence, because everything seems to be going in your favour. Your element luck is stellar, with all aspects of your luck rated very good or higher.

The **38 year old Water Dog** especially enjoys quite outstanding wealth luck – tycoon status is not out of the question. *Big Auspicious* comes from the direction of the Rooster, which indicates that those born under the Rooster sign bring very good luck to the Dog born, and collaborations between Dog and Rooster meet with great success in 2020.

The Rooster brings Big Auspicious Luck to the Dog in 2020.

Dealing with #7 in the CENTER

The #7 star in the center of the chart must be kept subdued at all costs if you want a peaceful and harmonious household in 2020.

In cosmic astrology, the ancients will refer to this as a year of the "Broken Soldier" which is the way the #7 star number is described.

It brings betrayal, violence and even bloodshed; and anger can easily descend into harmful and violent aggression. The 7 is a Metal Star and is controlled by the element of Water. From a feng shui perspective then, placing **Water** in the center of the house or the living room is highly recommended.

BLUE COLOUR SCHEME FOR THE CENTER: Note that the recommended colour scheme for the center of the home this year is blue; invest in blue scatter cushions with symbols of protection for the center of the home. You can also place a blue-coloured carpet or throw-rugs in the center of the living area to simulate the presence of the Water element.

We also recommend the following important remedies to keep the 7 well under control:

1. Place the **Blue Elephant & Rhino** with **Talisman Feathers** here. The Elephant and Rhino in blue, the colour of Water, remedies the Loss Star and this year we have designed this pair of guardians with talisman feathers for added protection. The pair also features the **Anti-Robbery Amulet** to keep the home insulated against robbers and intruders.

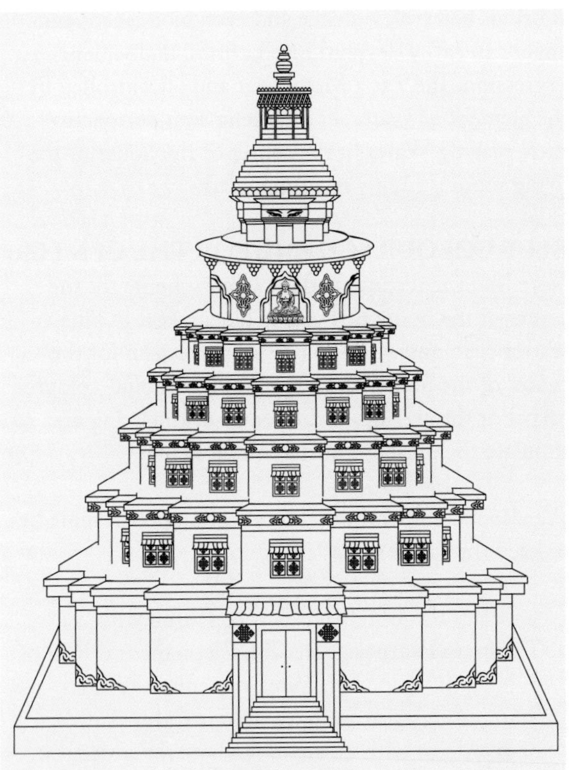

2. Display the **Kumbum Stupa** in the Center. The #7 star affects everyone this year. It requires the presence of a very strong sacred symbolic

cure to ensure families stay protected against its negative influences. The best spiritual remedy for the #7 is the Kumbum Stupa, which subdues all afflictions and ill energies, and invokes the protective presence of many Wisdom and Enlightened Protectors within the home.

This cure is especially important if any family member belongs to an animal sign that suffers from low life force or spirit essence this year.

The Kumbum Stupa transforms your home into a sacred abode so that malevolent influences cannot enter. It attracts multiple blessings that transform negative energies into positive ones, and ensures you do not suffer from unexpected or untoward reversals of fortune.

3. The presence of **King Gesar with the 13 Wermas** is another highly effective presence to have in the home this year. King Gesar is the Warrior Buddha who brings not just protection but

prosperity and material success. He is revered in all the lineage texts for his absolute triumph over evil and over one's rivals and enemies, and with his cortege of 13 Wermas (guardian animals), he protects against 13 kinds of danger. Place him in a respectful position in the center of your home, or on your altar.

4. We have also designed the **Blue Mongoose Carpet** to protect wealth and preserve one's family assets in a year dominated by the #7 Loss Star. Because the Loss Star appears in the center sector, its negative effects affect everyone. The Mongoose is the companion of the Wealth Buddhas and brings the symbolism of continued flows of income and expanding prosperity. Place this carpet in the center part of the home, or of any room you spend a lot of time in.

MAKE INCENSE OFFERINGS

Regular incense offerings go a long way to appeasing the local spirits around your home. This is our absolute favorite method of ensuring everything goes smoothly. When you light incense regularly, offering first to the Deities, then to the local spirits around your home, you can depend on their help to assist you in keeping your home and family safe from anyone with ill intentions even entering your home.

You can burn any kind of incense, but incense with white smoke is always best. We have put together a whole collection of incense on our website *www.fsmegamall.com* and in our World of Feng Shui stores for you to choose from. Because incense is such a beneficial remedy to so many things, we have worked hard at expanding our range for all kinds of homes and uses.

Select incense and incense burners that are easy for you to use on a daily basis. Incense also cleanses the air and infuses your living space with powerful and beneficial fragrances.

As you light your incense daily, pronounce the following invocation:

**NAMAH SARVA
TATHAGATHA AVALOKITE
OM SAMBHARA SAMBHARA HUNG**

Beware Quarrelsome Star #3 in the NORTH

This year, the NORTH, the sector of the ruling animal sign of the year the Rat, has the #3 Quarrelsome Star in residence.

The #3 is a Wood Star, and flying into Water element sector, it gets strengthened. Many feng shui masters

The Quarrelsome Star in the North gets strengthened this year and needs to be subdued.

believe that the #3 has the potential to wreak a lot more havoc than even the *Five Yellow* and other misfortune-bringing stars, and in 2020, because its potency gets enhanced, it is more vital than ever that you strongly suppress it. The #3 star brings conflict and misunderstanding, afflicting anyone born in the year of the Rat, as well as anyone whose bedroom, office or study is located in the North. It also affects all homes whose main door is located here, or anyone who spends a lot of time in this sector.

The NORTH part of all homes and living spaces must be kept as quiet as possible this year.

Keep anything that makes sound and noise out of this sector – this means that TVs, stereo systems and musical instruments should not occupy this sector this year; and definitely NO WINDCHIMES here.

CURE FOR THE NORTH

The best cure for the #3 this year is the **Fire Dragon Holding a Fireball.** This Fire Dragon has been designed in resplendent red studded with red jewels and holding Ksiddigarbha's Fireball, making it an effective and quick-acting cure for the negative effects of the #3.

The Dragon is also the astrological ally of the Rat, thus ensuring that any disagreeable energy manifesting in conflict and quarrels get not only suppressed but converted into harmonious interactions instead.

Place the Fire Dragon Holding Fireball in the North to suppress the Quarrelsome Star here.

This cure is especially vital for those facing legal problems or lawsuits, or those who are having difficulties dealing with the authorities. Having the Red Dragon with Fireball in the North will ensure the year goes smoothly and harmoniously for you, and insulate you against the ill effects of the #3.

Place the **Bejewelled Lucky Tortoise** in the North. There is nothing quite like the tortoise to generate unshakeable support luck and protection against harm from anyone who may wish to challenge you.

The tortoise signifies protective support for the home and ensures that residents stay strong and firm, no matter what trials and tribulations come their way.

In lineage texts, the tortoise was also the bearer of the magical Lo Shu square of numbers, which it was said to have carried to Fu Hsi with all the mysteries of feng shui. It is said to conceal within the design motifs on its shell all the secrets of heaven and earth.

Having the presence of the tortoise in the home ensures members of the household do not get harmed by ill flying star changes, protecting family members from illness, aggravations, quarrels and the ill intentions of others.

EAST plays host to the FIVE YELLOW

The other star everyone needs to be careful about is the *wu wang*, the Five Yellow.

This misfortune star flies to the East this year, affecting all those born under the sign of Rabbit, the eldest son and also, anyone whose homes face the East direction, or whose bedroom, office or study is located

The Five Yellow misfortune star occupies the East sector in 2020.

CHAPTER FOUR

here. The East being a Wood sector goes some way to moderating the influence of the Five Yellow, which is an Earth element star, as Wood destroys Earth. But we do not want to "destroy" the wu wang, we want to exhaust its energies, suppressing its hazardous nature while bringing it back to equilibrium.

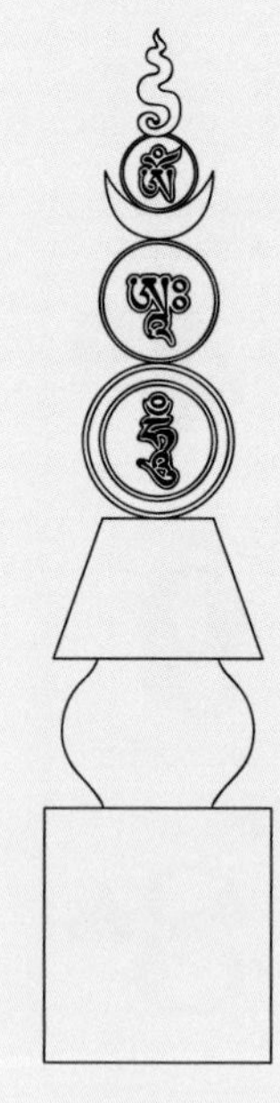

FIVE YELLOW CURE

This year's **Five Element Pagoda** has been designed with Om Ah Hum, representing the essence of body, speech and mind, filled with more mantras within the pagoda to purify all 3 vital aspects of the environment.

If you have a house that is more than one level, make sure you have a Five Element Pagoda on every floor. Remember to keep the East part of the home free from too much noise, and avoid renovating in this sector this year – no banging, no digging, no knocking, no stereos.

ILLNESS STAR made worse by Fire element of the SOUTH

The Illness Star 2 has flown into the South. This has the effect of strengthening it, as the South is a Fire element sector.

The Illness Star of 2020 gets strengthened by the Fire energy of the South.

The #2 being an Earth star gets stronger than ever; and its ill effects, when they afflict you becomes even

CHAPTER FOUR

more dangerous. It is vital to strongly suppress this star number 2 in 2020. All those living in houses facing South, those born in Horse years, and those whose bedrooms or offices are located in this sector need to pay attention to health issues this year. Avoid mosquito-infested areas, do not eat out as often, and avoid gardening during hours when bugs and mosquitoes come out.

The #2 star also brings increased risk of accidents, so those afflicted by this star need to take care when driving, travelling or when taking part in risky sports or activities.

It is recommended to **WEAR AN AMULET** at all times, and to carry the appropriate cures installed in the South of the home and the office. To protect against illness or if you are already sick or feeling unwell, carry the **Wu Lou Garuda Health Amulet**.

If you have elderly members of the family living in the home, it isespecially important to keep this star under control. Move elderly folk out of bedrooms located in the South for the year, and make sure you have ample cures and symbols of health and longevity in the home.

1. Display **Sau, the God of Longevity** with a pair of cranes and holding a Peach and Wu Lou.

Sau is one of the most popular Deities found in many Chinese homes because he symbolizes good health and a smooth and long life. He is one of the three Star Gods comprising Fuk, Luk and Sau, who together represent the triple aspirations of any family – that of wealth, health and happiness. When displayed as a set, they representa complete life, with the three key aspects needed for ultimate happiness and well-being.

But when the illness star of the year gets strengthened like it does in 2020, it is highly recommended to display Sau with all his symbols of longevity. This includes the Peach, said to contain the nectar of immortality, cranes which represent long life, and the Wu Lou, the gourd of good health that brings an abundance of blessings.

2. Display the **Garuda Bird**, the powerful celestial protector said to subdue illness, disease and spiritual attacks caused by nagas. The Garuda Bird can be displayed on its own, or it can be displayed with Kuan Yin, the Goddess of Mercy.

Anyone who is ill, elderly or frail will benefit from the presence of the Garuda in the home. And anyone who suspects they may be under spiritual attack, or the victim of some kind of black magic, should most definitely have the Garuda Bird in their presence at all times.

Prosperity Originates in the NORTHWEST this year
(bringing wealth luck to the Patriarch)

The wonderfully auspicious good fortune star of 8 has flown into the NORTHWEST, the sector that represents the PATRIARCH.

This is extremely beneficial for everyone, as good fortune bestowed on the patriarch leads to auspicious

The wealth star blesses the Patriarch or main breadwinner of the family.

CHAPTER FOUR

luck for the whole family. The NW sector represents the father, the leader and the heads of all households and organizations, and when the number 8 makes its home in this sector, it means the world will be blessed with good and noble leadership.

When this sector is properly activated, it ensures the father figure makes decisions that benefit all who come under him. In the home, the breadwinner will prosper, and in the office, the bosses and managers provide good leadership to their charges. When the #8 is in the NW, it becomes especially important to enhance because the NW is such an important sector, but more than that, the element of METAL of the North weakens the Earth element of the #8.

Earth element enhancers such as **crystal geodes** and **crystal balls** are very lucky placed in the NW this year.

FENG SHUI ENHANCERS FOR THE NW:

1. All houses that face Northwest benefit from the Prosperity Star this year. Activating this sector with **crystals** and **Earth-element enhancers** in 2020 bring double benefit, stimulating the wealth star and at the same time strengthening the luck of the patriarch. If your office or bedroom is located here, it further benefits you with new

prosperity flowing your way. Having a cluster of **6 smooth crystal balls** in the NW will ensure the luck of the patriarch continuously expands, as well as generating fabulously harmonious vibes throughout the home.

2. If you have windows in the NW corner, it is a good idea to hang **faceted crystal balls** in the windows. These will convert the light streaming through the window into rainbow light, which brings incredible blessings for the father and for the whole family.

WEALTH ENHANCERS FOR THE NW:

1. The image of a **Golden Rat Holding a Coin** with **"Your Luck Has Arrived"** is an excellent enhancer for the NW, as we are entering the Year of the Golden Rat. Of all the animal signs, the Rat is the most adaptable to change, and in these modern times when technology is moving at such a breakneck pace, the Rat is the best symbol to display if you want to take advantage of new and exciting opportunities opening up. With the Chinese, it is a well-loved tradition to display images of the Rat depicted with coins and ingots, especially in years of the Rat, when this animal is the ruling animal of the year. Remember that the RAT symbolizes having a continuance of wealth!

2. You can also place the **Rat Windchime for Wealth** in the NW. The tinkling sounds of metal on metal activates the wealth star here and also serves to strengthen the energies of the sector. An excellent energiser for this Year of the Rat!

3. Place **White Dzambala** in the NW. White Dzambala with his Azure Dragon and companion mongoose spouting jewels increases your streams of income and helps build wealth and career prospects. Dzambala is extremely powerful if you want to make the most of the Prosperity Star this year. Displaying White Dzambala in the home opens up the cosmic channels for wealth to flow freely into your life! You can also chant his mantra regularly for added potency:

OM PADMA KRODHA AYAH DZAMBALA HRIDAYA HUM PHAT

4. Display the **Rat & Dragon Prosperity "8"** in the NW. The animal sign of the year, the Rat, together with the Chinese Dragon, represents great wealth and prosperity for the coming year. The Rat is the sign that can forage for food and supplies no matter what the circumstances.

The mighty Dragon possesses the courage and confidence to take the big risks that reap the big rewards. Together, Rat and Dragon forming an 8 makes a fabulous wealth enhancer for the home this year.

5. Place the **Lucky Money Frog** on Waterlily Leaf here. The 3-legged money frog sitting on its natural habitat of a waterlily pad symbolizes a continuous flow of income into the household. Place in the NW to activate the wealth energies of the #8, or you can also place anywhere in the home.

6. Hang a **picture of the Patriarch** or main breadwinner of the household in the NW of the living room. This generates excellent feng shui for the whole family and ensures the father continues to prosper but more importantly, to feature prominently within the family. This makes sure all benefits accruing to the head of the household spills over to the entire family.

WEST represents Future Prosperity & Long-Term Gains

(for plans with a longer time-frame)

The West benefits from the presence of the #9 Future Prosperity Star in 2020. This star brings wealth that lasts into the long-term and indicates success for projects and plans with a longer time-frame.

SOUTHEAST	SOUTH	SOUTHWEST
6 *Heavenly Star*	2 THREE KILLINGS *Illness*	SCHOLASTIC LUCK 4 *Peach Blossom*
EAST	**CENTER**	**WEST**
5 WU WANG *Five Yellow*	7 BURGLARY *Violence*	9 *Completion*
NORTHEAST	**NORTH**	**NORTHWEST**
1 *Victory Luck*	TAI SUI 3 *Quarrelsome*	8 *Prosperity*

The West brings the luck of long-term gains and asset wealth in 2020.

The #9 is also a magnifying star, so its presence here injects passion and vibrancy to all homes facing West, to those who reside in rooms in the West, and to all born in Rooster years. The number 9 brings new vitality and renewed inspiration, boosting enthusiasm and creativity, and those whose job or purpose requires creativity, new ideas and strong imagination will benefit greatly from the auspicious winds brought by this star.

The only thing one needs to keep in mind is that when an unlucky month star makes an appearance in the WEST this year, the number 9 here can magnify their effects, making bad luck get worse.

In general the West is an extremely lucky sector in 2020; one just needs to be careful in the months of **May, July, September** and **October** when less auspicious stars make an appearance here. In these months, it is best to keep the West less active.

ACTIVATE THE WEST

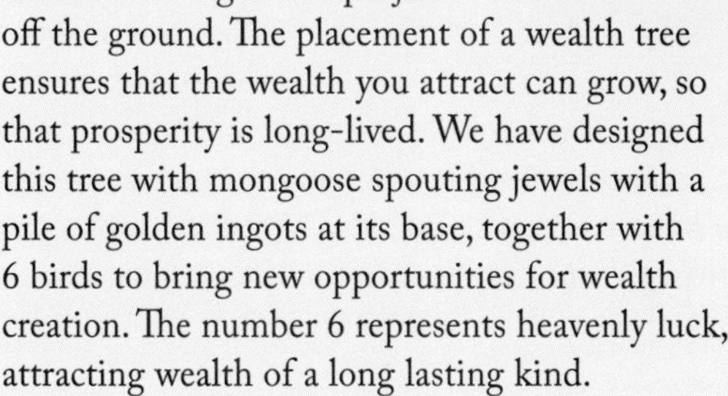

1. Place the **Wealth Tree with Mongoose & 6 Birds** in the West. This year 2020 has the presence of the Lap Chun which makes this a good year to get new ideas started and to get new projects off the ground. The placement of a wealth tree ensures that the wealth you attract can grow, so that prosperity is long-lived. We have designed this tree with mongoose spouting jewels with a pile of golden ingots at its base, together with 6 birds to bring new opportunities for wealth creation. The number 6 represents heavenly luck, attracting wealth of a long lasting kind.

When you have wealth luck on your side, it is important to also have opportunities that get that wealth to open up for you. This Wealth Tree enhancer ensures you get every chance to tap that prosperity luck. The mongoose brings the meaning that you can successfully transform all opportunities into riches, that your income streams will be continuous and your wealth can accumulate.

2. If promotion luck is what you want, display the **9 Rank Badges** tabletop enhancer in the West. This symbol brings career success and allows you to rise to the very top of whatever organization you work at. Those already at managerial level wishing to continue to rise up to a top position should also have the **Monkey sitting on an Elephant** in the West of the office or within sight on the workdesk.

3. Display a pair of **Wealth Cabinets** in the West. Wealth cabinets symbolise having surplus money that you can stow away and grow, ensuring you have not just enough to live on but plenty that you can use to safeguard your future. This year our wealth cabinets come in red and blue ornamented with golden ingots and coins. Red brings powerful yang energy and Blue is the colour of Water, the element that is always associated with money luck.

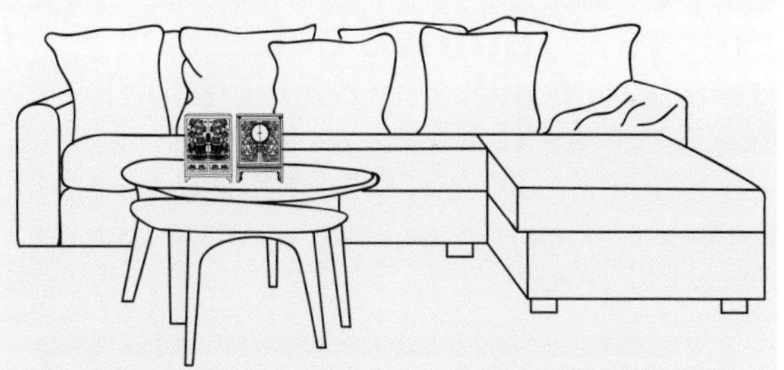

4. Displaying a **Rooster** in the West strengthens the energy of this sector. The Rooster is the epitome of vision, organization and punctuality. The Rooster also has the ability to peck away at productivity-quashing politicking and conflict. If your office is located in the West, make sure you have a Rooster on your work desk to ensure your path to success and promotion stays free of interference from rivals who may want to take your place.

NORTHEAST
enjoys Winning Luck
(*to triumph over any competition*)

The Victory Star #1 flies into the Northeast this year, benefitting all homes facing NE, anyone whose bedroom or office is located here, and those born in Ox and Tiger years.

The NE sector brings "winning" luck in 2020.

The NE is an Earth sector, so the #1 Water Star needs strengthening in the NE, in order to enjoy the full brilliance of its effects. But the presence of the *Winning Star* makes this a very lucky part of any home or premise.

The luck it brings allows one to triumph over any competition, so whenever you find yourself in a situation where you have to compete with others for recognition, business or good will, the energy of this sector helps you along.

1. The best enhancer for this year's #1 Victory Star is the **Windhorse-Boosting Victory Flag**. This flag comes with the King Gesar Mantra with all 5 element colours featured. This enhancer ensures you not only survive the competition but triumph over it in outstanding manner. Vital for anyone who has rivals of any kind.

2. Place the **Luo Han with Crab** in the NE. The Luo Han with Crab is one of the well-known 18

CHAPTER FOUR

Chinese Saints who bring good fortune in their distinctive forms. The Luo Han with Crab helps by bringing you excellent strategic thinking. It helps all entrepreneurs and executives make all the right decisions.

Having the Luo Han with Crab in the home imbues one with formidable intellect and great strategy and allows whoever taps on his power to rise up to high positions of rank and influence. All those with ambitions in the corporate field should have this Luo Han nearby. Place in the NE this year.

3. **Liu Bei**, the founder of the Shu-Han Dynasty during the Three Kingdom Periods is another extremely effective and auspicious symbol for the NE. Liu Bei was famous for bringing peace and prosperity to China during the Han Dynasty and well-known for his superior intellect and strategic acumen. Fantastic enhancer for the NE in 2020.

Invite into your home the great warrior Liu Bei to boost victory luck in any competitive endeavour.

SOUTHEAST
is blessed by the Heavens
(as well as Big Auspicious)

The Heavenly Star #6 flies into the Southeast, the sector of the Dragon and Snake. These two animal signs benefit from this star's benevolent influence, which means more opportunities coming their way, and more people working behind the scenes helping them.

SOUTHEAST	SOUTH	SOUTHWEST
6 BIG AUSPICIOUS *Heavenly Star*	2 THREE KILLINGS *Illness*	SCHOLASTIC LUCK 4 *Peach Blossom*
EAST	**CENTER**	**WEST**
5 WU WANG *Five Yellow*	7 BURGLARY *Violence*	9 *Completion*
NORTHEAST	**NORTH**	**NORTHWEST**
1 *Victory Luck*	TAI SUI 3 *Quarrelsome*	8 *Prosperity*

The Southeast enjoys blessings from heaven.
Activate with Jade Emperor with Qui Ren Talisman.

The Heaven Star also brings superior mentor and benefactor luck, so whatever the path you set out on, you will find bounteous help and assistance along the way.

When you enjoy the benefits of the #6 star, even if a path does not seem well-defined, you can have the confidence to venture forth, because things will have their own way of falling into place. All those living in homes facing SE, or whose bedroom or office is located in the SE will benefit from this star directly. Every home should make every endeavour to keep this part of the house active and filled with life. Do not "lock up" this auspicious star in some store room!

The SE is also the place of the eldest daughter of the family, who benefits from the cosmic luck of the heavens this year.

ACTIVATE THE HEAVEN STAR

1. Place the **Wealth Bull** in the SE. The Wealth Bull is the sacred buffalo of the Buddhas who bestows heightened spiritual perception and understanding, allowing you to spot the big opportunities when they come your way. It gives you the wisdom and the self-assuredness you will need to make the best decisions in all situations.

When you have the Wealth Bull on your side, it makes you invincible to enemies and strong in the face of competition. It gives you the will and

the savvy to make the most of all your openings, allowing you to turn Big Auspicious into big breaks. It infuses you with the energies of big success, makes you feel more alive and is the best enhancer for anyone with low levels of life force or spirit essence.

Its **deep blue colour** represents the Water element, which syncs nicely with the Wood element chi of the SE.

2. For business success, display the **Double Humped Camel**. This symbol is a must-have for anyone in business as it ensures you always maintain a healthy cash flow.

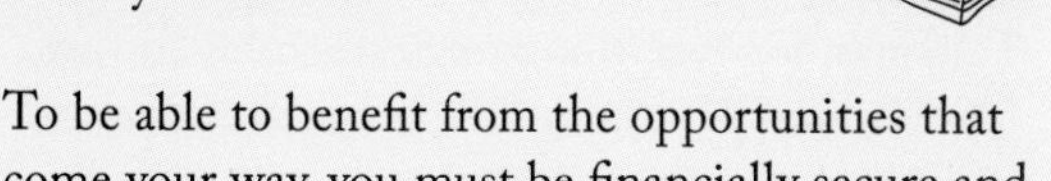

To be able to benefit from the opportunities that come your way, you must be financially secure and have a large enough war chest to ensure you can weather any turbulence ortemporary downturn in luck. Having the Double Humped Camel in your vicinity brings the qualities of steadfastness and financial security. It will ensure you can take the risks you need to take to make it really big!

3. All those whose bedrooms are located in the SE should carry or wear the **Lock Coin Amulet.** While there are big opportunities coming, the appearance of the *Robbery Star* from the 24 Mountains warns of danger of loss. Ensure all your risks are calculated and do not bite off more than you can chew. One step at a time is the way forward; then build on each step. Don't try to get ahead of yourself.

4. Display the **Jade Emperor with Qui Ren Talisman** for everything to go smoothly for you. Place in the SE sector of the home to capture all of heaven's auspicious blessings.

Peach Blossom Luck in the SOUTHWEST

(brings marriage opportunities)

Love and romance is in the air in the Southwest this year! The Peach Blossom Star #4 makes an appearance here and because this is also the Universal Love Corner as following the original Lo Shu pattern of the Yang Pa Kua, this makes its potency all the more effective!

SOUTHEAST	SOUTH	SOUTHWEST
6 *Heavenly Star*	2 THREE KILLINGS *Illness*	4 *Peach Blossom*
EAST	**CENTER**	**WEST**
5 WU WANG *Five Yellow*	7 BURGLARY *Violence*	9 *Completion*
NORTHEAST	**NORTH**	**NORTHWEST**
1 *Victory Luck*	TAI SUI 3 *Quarrelsome*	8 *Prosperity*

The Peach Blossom Star flies into the SW, bringing marriage opportunities.

Anyone living in the SW of homes has the potential to find love and to get married, if that is what you want!

The Peach Blossom Star makes you more sociable and more attuned to romance and romantic inclinations. It will make anyone residing in this sector more amenable to love and to matters of the heart.

The Southwest is also the sector of the Sheep and Monkey, so this year, these two animal signs benefit from enhanced opportunities for marriage and settling down. Those of marriageable age and looking for a partner should step up their efforts this year.

ENHANCING FOR LOVE IN THE SW:

1. If you are looking for a partner, place the **Red Tara Home Amulet** in the SW of your home. Filled with her precious mantras and then sealed, having her in the home invokes her sacred qualities and her presence. One of the manifestations of Red Tara is *Kurukulle,* the ultimate female Buddha with the power to help all those in

search of love and a soulmate. She improves your relationships with friends, colleagues, bosses and anyone else you deal with, and attracts true love into your life.

2. You can also display the **Banner of Love** featuring **Kurukulle,** the beautiful Goddess of Love. When shown holding her bow and arrow made of flowers, she is powerful indeed. Invoking her help boosts one's magnetism and charisma. If you have her image in the home and regularly call on her help, you will start to find everyone becoming friendlier towards you, bonding with you better, and your words and opinions will start counting for more in all discussions and discourses you have.

3. For those who wish to attract marriage opportunities into your life, or who wish to rekindle a tired marriage, display the **Double Happiness Symbol** or carry in your pocketas a gold wallet card.

4. For the already married, there is no better symbol than **Marriage Happiness Ducks**. These colourful ducks bring not just marital happiness; they light up your life and help you see all the beauty and good qualities in each other. They also subdue disharmony energies that cause quarrels and arguments. Essential symbol for the home of any married couple, as it ensures you stay happily married. It strengthens your love for one another and brings plenty of joy and good times to the marriage.

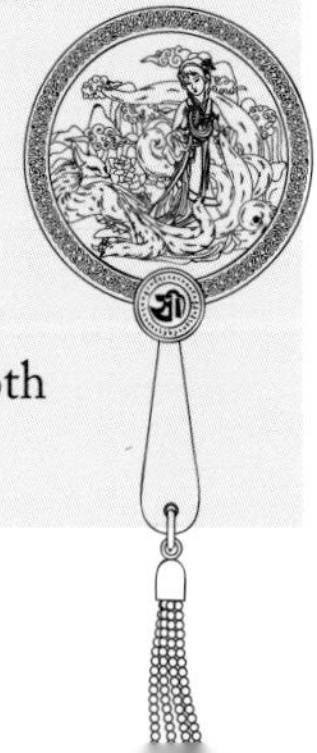

5. If you are looking for love and have your eye on someone, carry the **9-Tailed White Fox Amulet** to make you irresistible. This amulet will smooth your path to happiness in love.

SOUTHWEST
also brings scholastic success
(for students & those taking exams)

The #4 star also brings scholastic and academic Success. Those who benefit from the Peach Blossom aspects of this star will likewise benefit from the potential for scholastic achievements it bestows. Young Sheep and Monkey children in school benefit from study luck this year.

SOUTHEAST	SOUTH	SOUTHWEST
6 *Heavenly Star*	2 THREE KILLINGS *Illness*	SCHOLASTIC LUCK 4 *Peach Blossom*
EAST	**CENTER**	**WEST**
5 WU WANG *Five Yellow*	7 BURGLARY *Violence*	9 *Completion*
NORTHEAST	**NORTH**	**NORTHWEST**
1 *Victory Luck*	TAI SUI 3 *Quarrelsome*	8 *Prosperity*

The SW is excellent for students this year.
Brings exam success and scholastic accolades.

The #4 also brings greater creativity to those in lines of work that involve research, knowledge accumulation and application of that knowledge. The creativity imbues you with greater ability to think outside the box, so you do not just learn up knowledge but add to it.

1. Place the **Scholar on Dragon Carp** in the SW. Shown with the *four symbols of scholarship*, this activator brings exam success and top academic attainment to those pursuing exams. To the Chinese, the Dragon Carp is the ultimate symbol of achievement and the 4 Scholastic Objects – the book, scroll, brush and flute – represent a balanced and well-rounded education. All homes with children of school or college-going age should have this symbol placed in the SW of the house or of their study room this year.

2. For children finding it difficult to get or stay motivated in studies, we recommend the **Red Wisdom Pagoda.** This pagoda generates enthusiasm and self-discipline, ensuring teenagers and young adults do not get side-tracked into unproductive activities, and do not fall under the influence of unsuitable company. Place in the SW of the home or study room of your teenager.

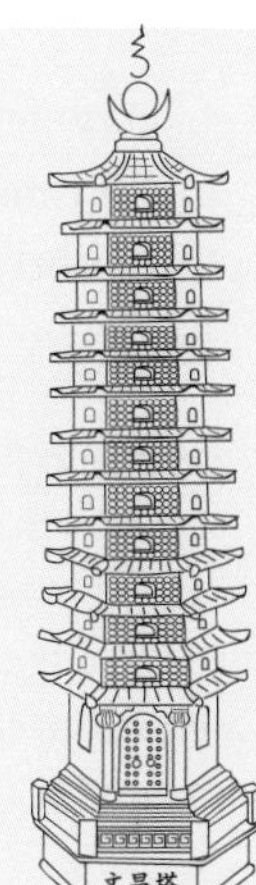

3. If you wish to call on spiritual help, invite in **Manjushri, the Buddha of Wisdom and Knowledge** into your home. He cuts through ignorance and brings understanding to all who seek it. Students pursuing top exam grades can call on his help to invoke his blessings. Place on an altar in the home or in a respectable place in

the SW in 2020. You can also wear the **Wealth and Wisdom Mantra Ring** which features Manjushri's mantra on the inside and Dzambala's mantra on the outside.

Learn up Manjushri's mantra and chant 108 times each day. Best to get a dedicated mala if you can. Whenever trying to access knowledge that's at the edge of your consciousness, e.g. in an exam situation, chant his mantra and let him bring the answer to you.

OM AH RA PA CHA NA DHI

Afflictions to watch out for...
TAI SUI in the North

Tai Sui or Grand Duke Jupiter, also known as the God of the Year, assists the Jade Emperor in helping and controlling the mortal world. The Tai Sui is usually regarded as the *Heavenly General*, although his personality, disposition and position within the compass changes from year to year.

Tai Sui resides in the North in 2020.

CHAPTER FOUR

In 2020, TAI SUI resides in the NORTH, the place of the Rat. This bestows on all those born under the sign of RAT his heavenly blessings and protection.

However, the animal sign directly opposite the Rat, i.e. the HORSE, usually risks thefull wrath of the Tai Sui as this is deemed to be confronting this powerful Year God. Many Taoists also believe that it is not just the animal sign directly facing the Tai Sui of the year that risks offending the Tai Sui. All four animals that form a cross with the conflicting animal sign are at risk.

In 2020 therefore, the cardinal animals of **Horse, Rabbit, Rooster** and **Rat** all need to be mindful that they take steps to appease the Tai Sui. Especially the HORSE, who directly confronts the Tai Sui!

To get Tai Sui onto your side, we always recommend having a pair of **heavenly Pi Yao** in his location – in 2020, place a pair of Pi Yao in the North. You should also place the **image of the year's Tai Sui** here.

We have made his image into a plaque to display in the home, and also as a portable amulet to carry throughout the day. Note that the Tai Sui changes each year, and in all, there are 60 Tai Sui. It is important to pay attention to this important dimension of your feng shui update each year.

THREE KILLINGS in the South

The Three Killings can be a troublesome affliction when you ignore it, because it brings 3 kinds of losses – loss of wealth, loss of your good name and reputation, and loss of someone you love.

The 3 Killings cause troubles to come not in ones and twos but, as Shakespeare said, in "battalions" - resembling a 3-pronged attack at three important dimensions of happiness.

In 2020, this affliction enters the SOUTH, anyone whose house faces South, or whose bedroom or

The Three Killings resides in the South in 2020, bringing 3 kinds of bad luck. It MUST be suppressed.

office is located South will be affected by its negative energies. This is an important affliction to control, because its effects can be devastatingly severe. It is important to keep it under control.

This year we recommend the **Three Celestial Bells** featuring the three guardians – the Pi Yao, Chi Lin and Fu Dog. Bells of this size and shape are powerful cures; they also signify achievement in the face of great obstacles.

The symbolism of the bells is truly powerful as the sound of these bells completely annihilates all bad vibrations, especially those caused by the 3 Killings affliction. These bells also protect you from bad intentions aimed your way by those jealous of your success or situation.

Do NOT have your back to the SOUTH this year. This means you MUST NOT face North even if it is a "good" direction for you according to your Kua. Doing so could cause you to get "hit" by the Three Killings!

Place the 3 Celestial Bells in the South sector this year to suppress the Three Killings.

CHAPTER 5

DOG INTERACTING WITH OTHERS IN 2020

DOG'S RELATIONSHIPS WITH OTHER SIGNS IN 2020

Dog's good-natured personality earns you a lot of friends this year

To the Chinese, especially when searching for a marriage partner, few things matter more to a bride or groom's parents than compatibility of horoscopes between their child and the potential partner. Indeed, when match-making, the first thing one would look at are the animal signs of the potential couple and further to that, the Paht Chee charts of the couple.

When you look at not just the year of birth but all four pillars of birth, superficial incompatibilities can be overcome, just like seeming dream pairings may not be all that first meets the eye. Understanding how all this works helps one ensure that any partnership you enter into stands the best chance of harmony, success and longevity.

In today's world, it is not just marriage where astrological compatibilities are investigated. One can use these methods to ensure a new employee can get along with the team, to examine pros and cons before entering a joint venture, or even which friends you can trust more than others.

For couples having children, planning the best years to conceive can boost chances of siblings getting along nicely, children staying filial to their parents and bringing honour, pride and happiness to the family.

SHORT VS LONG RUN COMPATIBILITY

While major compatibilities (and mismatches) tend to hold true in the longer run, the nuances of relationships nevertheless ebb and flow and change from year to year. When one is going through a good year, it makes it easier to get along with others in general. Natural affinity gets enhanced and incompatibilities are reduced when stars align in your favour.

In the short term, while two animal signs may not jive well following the traditional understanding of horoscopes, their luck patterns may merge nicely for a particular year, which enables them to achieve success when they team up. This kind of fluctuating compatibility is useful when checking whether or not to join forces for a short-term project, or to team up for a set transitory period. Understanding how relationship affinities fluctuate will also help you avoid getting stuck with someone who is evidently unsuited to you, but who you may fall head over heels over in the short term. When warned not to let things get too serious, you may want to hold out and test a particular relationship a little longer before committing to say marriage or a formal business partnership.

Being aware of the tones and gradations of astrological compatibilities will also allow you to understand people's reactions better, which will let you improve relations with those already in your life whether you like it or not.

Gaining a solid understanding of feng shui astrology gives you practical methods to nullify any relationship afflictions you may face.

For instance, if you are already married with children but struggling to keep the peace in the marriage, there are remedies that can make your already existing union more harmonious.

In this chapter, we discuss all the major compatibilities to take note of, and then we look at the DOG and its compatibility with each of the 12 different animal signs in 2020.

COMPATIBILITY GROUPINGS

1. TRIANGLES OF AFFINITY - *great support*
2. ASTROLOGICAL SOULMATES - *power friendship*
3. SECRET FRIENDS - *influencing each other*
4. SEASONAL TRINITIES - *wealth-enhancing*
5. PEACH BLOSSOM LINKS - *romance*
6. YOUR ZODIAC ENEMY - *astrological foes*

1. TRIANGLES OF AFFINITY

There are four triangles of affinity made up of three animals signs. Each grouping possesses similar traits, reactions and belief systems that create natural bonds between them. Their thought processes are similar, and their aims and life goals coincide. When you belong to the same triangle of affinity, you are bound to get along well and be naturally supportive of one another.

Animal signs that belong to the same affinity triangle are set four years apart, and when planning to have children, a good way to ensure they all get along is to plan a four-year age gap between them.

The four sets of affinity triangles are as follows:

COMPETITORS Rat, Dragon, Monkey	Ambitious, Brilliant, Tough
THINKERS Ox, Snake, Rooster	Generous, Focused, Resilient
ADVENTURERS Dog, Tiger, Horse	Ethical, Brave, Loyal
DIPLOMATS Boar, Sheep, Rabbit	Creative, Kind, Emotional

The DOG belongs to the affinity triangle of ADVENTURERS, together with the HORSE and TIGER. You are the independents of the Chinese Zodiac always looking for the next adventure. You are happiest when on the move, and travel will be high on your list of priorities. You love to explore the world and prefer visiting new destinations than to keep returning to a favourite vacation spot. You collect experiences rather than things, and you treasure good memories in good company. You are highly sociable and make new friends easily. For this group, once acquaintances become pals, you prove your loyalty many times over to each other.

When someone of the DOG sign gets together with a HORSE or TIGER, you will have found your fellow free spirit, your ideal companion to soak up all the world has to offer. You value dependability in your relationships; and you give it in return.

When you embark on a relationship with someone from your own affinity triangle, yours will be a union full of exhilarating escapades and new experiences, full of fun, dynamism and vigour.

2. ASTROLOGICAL SOULMATES

There are six pairs of soulmates in the Chinese Zodiac, with each pair creating a special talent when they come together. It is easy to find happiness in the arms of your soulmate. In each pair, a yin generates perfect balance with its yang counterpart. Each pair is known as a Zodiac House, and within each pair, a very special cosmic bond is created when they come together. Any marriage, business partnership or friendship between two signs from the same house results in a relationship whose sum is greater than its individual parts.

The DOG and BOAR form the *House of Domesticity*. Their *forte* when they come together is to build a blissful family life that is not just picture perfect, but skin deep. They are genuinely happy together, with neither in the relationship for any other reason than that they truly love or care for one another.

When Dog meets Boar, there is instant chemistry, and it is very easy for even platonic pals to become more than just friends. This pairing works whatever the nature of their relationship, but their shared aspiration will be happiness rather than prosperity, appreciating the smaller but more significant aspects of life together.

ANIMALS	YIN/ YANG	ZODIAC HOUSE CREATED	TALENTS UNLEASHED
RAT & OX	YANG/ YIN	**House of Creativity and Cleverness**	The Rat initiates The Ox completes
TIGER & RABBIT	YANG/ YIN	**House of Growth and Development**	The Tiger uses strength The Rabbit uses negotiation
DRAGON & SNAKE	YANG/ YIN	**House of Magic and Spirituality**	The Dragon takes action The Snake creates magic
HORSE & SHEEP	YANG/ YIN	**House of Passion and Sexuality**	The Horse embodies strength & courage The Sheep embodies seduction & allure
MONKEY & ROOSTER	YANG/ YIN	**House of Career and Commerce**	The Monkey creates good strategy The Rooster takes timely action
DOG & BOAR	YANG/ YIN	**House of Domesticity**	The Dog creates alliances The Boar benefits

Table of Astrological Soulmates

3. SECRET FRIENDS

There are six pairs of secret friends in the Chinese Zodiac and they are extraordinarily compatible. When they become lovers or friends, they genuinely have each other's best interests at heart. There is no malice, no rivalry and no distrust at all.

> Secret friends need no acknowledgement when they help each other out, hence their namesake.

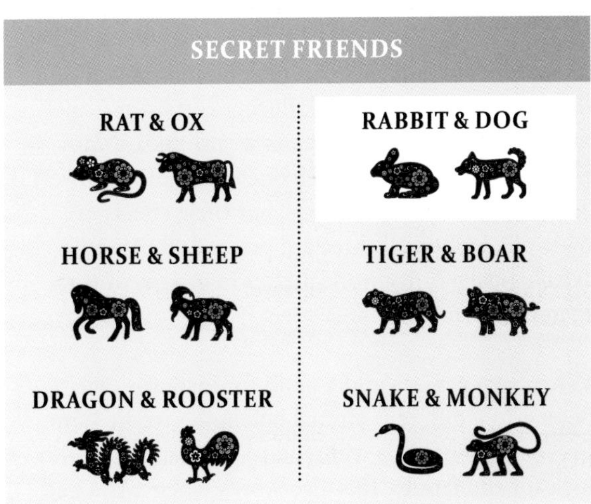

For the DOG, your secret friend the RABBIT is someone who will help you out even without your knowing. When taking advice from your secret friend, you can be sure they have no ulterior motive when offering their opinion. There is a lot of trust between secret friends. Dog takes the lead from Rabbit's eloquency and way with words, while Rabbit benefits from Dog's unwavering loyalty. For the Rabbit, the Dog is the perfect cheerleader; and for the Dog, the Rabbit lights the way. Each sign should display their secret friend in the home to boost the power of this pairing.

4. SEASONAL GROUPINGS

There are four seasonal trinity combinations of signs that bring exceptional luck during certain seasons. Such luck usually manifests as wealth luck. Many experts consider these to be one of the more powerful combination of animal signs, but their effects are multiplied when all three are present. Hence this astrological affinity works better in groups of three than between couples.

When two parents and a child for instance each belong to a different animal belonging to the same Seasonal group, this will tend to manifest as wealth luck for the family. This also works when a trio get together for a business or commercial venture – their affinity manifests as mutual success for all three.

It is necessary for all three to live together or work in the same office in close proximity for the pattern of prosperity to take effect. For greater impact, it is better if all are using the direction associated with the relevant seasons. Thus the seasonal combination of Spring is East, while the seasonal combination of Summer is South.

The table below summarises the seasonal groupings.

ANIMALS	SEASON	ELEMENT/ DIRECTION
Dragon, Rabbit, Tiger	Spring	Wood/East
Snake, Horse, Sheep	Summer	Fire/South
Monkey, Rooster, Dog	Autumn	Metal/West
Ox, Rat, Boar	Winter	Water/North

The Monkey, Rooster and Dog belong to the seasonal grouping of Autumn.

The DOG belongs to the seasonal combination of Autumn, which strengthens its links with the Monkey and Rooster. When a Dog and Monkey marry and they have a Rooster child for instance, the three together form the Trinity of Autumn. This means they are not only exceptionally close but attract the luck of wealth and abundance during the autumn season.

5. PEACH BLOSSOM LINKS

Each of the alliances of allies has a special relationship with one of the four primary signs of Horse, Rat, Rooster and Rabbit. These are the symbolic representations of love and romance for one alliance group of animal signs. In the horoscope, they are referred to as Peach Blossom Animals and the presence of their image in the home of the matching alliance of allies brings Peach Blossom Luck, which symbolizes love and romance.

The DOG belongs to the alliance of Dog, Tiger and Horse, and for them, the RABBIT is their Peach Blossom Animal.

Placing a **Peach Blossom Rabbit** in the East sector of the home or bedroom will activate love and romance for the Dog, attracting marriage opportunities for you.

6. YOUR ZODIAC ENEMY

There is a six year gap between natural enemies. A marriage between them is not usually recommended. When you get together with your Zodiac enemy, it will be difficult for you to make your union last because there are so many inherent infidelities. Zodiac enemies, even if you start out as the best of friends or the most infatuated of lovers, will tend to fall out or grow apart over time. You are not inherently suited to one another, so the advice is not to start anything serious in the first place.

ZODIAC ENEMY	
RAT & HORSE	RABBIT & ROOSTER
OX & SHEEP	TIGER & MONKEY
DRAGON & DOG	SNAKE & BOAR

Do not leave yourself vulnerable to your zodiac enemy, because they can hurt you without even meaning to. Indeed, arguments and fall-outs between zodiac foes have far longer-lasting effects than any other pairs of animal signs. Differences are magnified, and conflicts are uglier.

The DOG'S Zodiac Enemy is the DRAGON, so it is best for Dog to not get too close to anyone of the Dragon sign. In a marriage, this union is unlikely to bring lasting happiness unless other indications in their Paht Chee or other charts suggest otherwise. In a business partnership, this pairing is likely to lead to problems, sometimes ending in lengthy litigation and plenty of bad blood.

Dog & Dragon will never be happily compatible. This is a pairing that might work in the early stages of a relationship, but that gets extremely acromonious and untenably damaging as time takes its course.

ENEMY REMEDY: If you are already in some kind of relationship with your Zodiac enemy, the best remedy is to display the secret friend of your astrological enemy. For the DOG in a relationship with a DRAGON, you should display the secret friend of the Dragon, i.e. the **Rooster sitting on an astrological pillar** near you.

ANNUAL INFLUENCES
to the Horoscope Compatibilities

Annual energies affect what kind of people you have greater or lesser affinity with. In some years, you could feel an inexplicable aversion to someone you have always liked and loved; or a sudden attraction to someone you have always found infuriating!

Usually, affinity groupings, secret friend alliances and soulmate pairings of the Zodiac exert strong influences, but annual chi energy changes also have the power to influence your thinking and the way you behave or react to others. These changes can make you more argumentative or more affectionate, more impatient or more considerate.

Personal luck also influences how we act around others. When life and work goes well, we become better disposed to those in our orbit. When luck is riding high, even a Zodiac enemy can become a friend, even if only for a short period of time.

Likewise, when one is being challenged by major problems or obstacles, even the slightest provocation can lead to anger. Even Zodiac friends and allies might then appear to be insufferable. A falling-out between horoscope allies is thus not impossible when the energies go against you.

In this section, we examine the DOG's personal relationships with the other signs in 2020.

DOG'S RELATIONSHIPS WITH OTHER SIGNS IN 2020

PAIRINGS	COMPATIBILITY IN 2020
DOG & RAT	Ho Tu combination brings good fortune
DOG & OX	Dog puts more into the relationship
DOG & TIGER	Natural compatibility results in lasting love
DOG & RABBIT	A cosy and comfortable relationship
DOG & DRAGON	Astrological foes find common ground in 2020
DOG & SNAKE	Lopsided match but some chemistry in 2020
DOG & HORSE	Allies enjoying sum-of-ten luck
DOG & SHEEP	Better when Dog takes the lead
DOG & MONKEY	Little in common but love can be found in 2020
DOG & ROOSTER	Unexpected pairing but may work in 2020
DOG & DOG	Meeting with much success together in 2020
DOG & BOAR	An enduring couple having a great year!

DOG/RAT *love blossoms*

Ho Tu combination brings good fortune

The Dog and Rat, while not the most passionate of couples, enjoy a quiet and contented kind of relationship with one another. While sparks are unlikely to fly between these two, should they get together as a couple, it will not be difficult for them to make things last.

The Dog is an Earth animal, happiest when sniffing out new adventures, and with loved ones, loyal to a fault. Rat is far more shrewd and wily, and Dog's holier-than-thou ways could sometimes grate on Rat's nerves. But in 2020, love gets every chance to blossom because their star numbers combine to form the magical *Ho Tu!*

In 2020, Dog and Rat find they have more in common than they may have at first thought. Rat learns to appreciate Dog's dedicated do-gooder ways, while Dog takes a walk on the wild side with the street-smart Rat. Rat's #3 and Dog's #8 bring out a trendsetting trait in them, and together they could well become the hottest couple in town! This year, Dog and Rat enjoy the social scene together and become the life of any party with no effort at all. Rat's argumentative nature gets totally subdued when together with the happy-go-lucky Dog, while Dog's self-confidence grows in the company of the Rat. Both benefit from the influence of the other, making this a good pairing whether in love, work or play.

Dog and Rat at work will see Dog take charge this year, as the Dog is feeling far stronger and more energised than the Rat. Rat is happy to let Dog take the lead as long as Dog does not expect Rat to lift too many fingers. They are compatible in 2020 as both adopt some of the other's personality traits. Their outlooks jive, if only temporarily, but there is enough time for many wonderful shared experiences and successes.

Whether Dog and Rat can last the long haul is another matter. The Earth element of the Dog will ultimately harm the Water element of the Rat. They are not naturally compatible. If you are looking for short term fun, or getting involved for a project with a definite term period, by all means go ahead with no holds barred. But if you are thinking of marriage, be sure you are truly compatible before taking the plunge, or you could find yourself locked into what each considers a dull union.

DOG/OX *one-sided*

Dog puts more into the relationship

While not a naturally compatible pair, 2020 sees these two strike a good balance with each other, so should they come together in this Year of the Rat, Dog and Ox can enjoy a successful and happy time with one another. Both are Earth element animals, and both enjoy excellent indications from the year's charts.

Ox has the *Victory Star* on its side, while Dog enjoys wealth luck. Their element luck charts are also very promising, so while each is having a jolly good time, there is very little to disagree about and they see only the good in each other.

As partners in love, Dog & Ox are not a wildly passionate pair. Theirs is a restrained relationship where they are comfortable with each other, but with little excitement. What thrills they get will come from the interests they pursue together. If they have mutual friends and hobbies, theirs can be a contented and easy-going union.

But because there is little natural chemistry, there is always the danger of one or the other of them

straying from the relationship. The risk of this lies more with the Ox, who is not so fiercely loyal as the Dog.

In this relationship, it will always be the Dog trying harder and putting in more effort. But the sad thing is not the harder the Dog tries, the more unimpressed the Ox becomes. Ox may start to take Dog for granted, and do silly things that can be quite unforgivable, yet Dog will try to forgive and forget. Until it doesn't.

In 2020, Ox has the upper hand with a powerful ally in the year's dominant Rat energy, so Dog will find itself having to give in over and over. But for now, Dog seems happy to do so. Ox is preoccupied with work and career matters, and meeting with success, it has with little time to indulge in its philandering ways. Dog meanwhile enjoys its own set of professional achievements, so in love and relationship matters, Dog is happy to pander to Ox's whims.

For the married couple, a Dog and Ox relationship will not always be smooth. Ox has the tendency to bring out all that is growly in the Dog, but this union can last because Dog will always give in to the Ox. Happily, 2020 will see a much rosier time for this pair as both are going through a good year.

DOG/TIGER ***astrological allies***

Natural compatibility results in true love

The Dog and Tiger are always good together, and this becomes even more so in this Year of the Rat when both enjoy extremely fortunate element luck indications with excellent feng shui winds blowing their way. They are astroligical allies whose temperaments and aspirations jive so well together. With Tiger and Dog, they have much natural affinity, and even though both have a temper, they rarely lose it with one another.

In 2020, Dog & Tiger bring out all that is loving in each other. They make an affectionate couple who boosts each other's *joie de vivre* and lust for life. When together, the world is their oyster and they enjoy many happiness moments together.

Ths year, Tiger has victory luck, so comes out on top in any competitive situation. With a Dog partner by its side, it feels empowered and secure, while Dog also enjoys many successes of its own. Both are extremely loyal, and rarely can an outsider do anything to shake their enduring bond. In 2020, both Dog and Tiger enjoy very fortunate element luck indications, so neither actually needs the other for strength or moral

support; yet both give it freely in this relationship, and none of it goes unappreciated.

While with others, the Dog can have a fierce growl, and the Tiger an intimidating roar, with each other they revert to their affectionate selves, becoming quite the puppy and the pussycat. They are indulgent of one another, and however things may be playing out in their careers, they always make time for each other.

As a romantic pairing, they are generous lovers and continue to mesmerize each other for years to come. In work, if they start out having good rapport, they turn that into a productive union almost immediately. These are Zodiac allies that always stay true to one another, and when they commit to one another, they truly become each other's best friends. There is a lot of trust flowing between them and they always give each other the benefit of the doubt.

This year, both Dog and Tiger enjoy success in their own respective fields, but both appreciate the moral support the other gives. Should they be working together in the same field, the results are even more spectacular. A match made in heaven indeed!

DOG/RABBIT *secret friends*

A cosy and comfortable relationship

These two have a very special connection because they are *secret friends* of the Chinese Zodiac. Theirs is the kind of union where they are instantly comfortable in each other's company and always have each other's best interests at heart.

With a Dog, Rabbit does not feel it needs to prove itself, so it gets off its high horse and becomes a lot more tolerable. With a Rabbit, Dog finds a partner that repays its fierce loyalty with just as much devotion, so there is little danger of either getting the seven-year itch or developing a roving eye, no matter what kind of temptation gets thrust their way.

The Dog and Rabbit may not have the most explosive of starts, but should they develop enough love to marry, theirs will be a long-lasting, happy and fulfilling union.

They make an ideal match because of their highly compatible personalities. Both are even-tempered and reasonable, and neither will allow a small disagreement to escalate into any kind of fight. They resolve conflicts in highly adult manner, keeping cool and calm in all situations.

★★★★★

To others they may come across a rather dull and boring pair, with little day-to-day drama, but their deeply endearing love more than makes up for any lack of fireworks.

As work mates, these two are highly productive when they join forces, and while money will rarely be apriority in whatever they are doing, they could end up making quite a lot of it together!

In 2020, Dog has the *Prosperity Star* in its sector, so whatever it puts its efforts towards will tend to meet with decent commercial success. While Rabbit's luck may not be so stellar with the *Five Yellow* to contend with, it has superlative element luck indications, suggesting it can be a most useful ally for the Dog. Because of their respective luck indications, it is better for Dog to take the lead, but the amiable Rabbit is more than happy for this to be the case.

The best thing about a Dog and Rabbit pairing is that they really do have genuine affection for one another. They are protective of each other, and while both can be selfish when it comes to others, with each other, they put the other first. There is much love here that goes way beyond just romance. An enviable match!

DOG/DRAGON *better this year*

Astrological foes who find common ground in 2020

Dog and Dragon are natural adversaries of the Zodiac and it would be highly unlikely for Dog and Dragon to even be attracted to one another in the first place. From the start, each finds the other irksome and exasperating, and theirs will be a very superficially cordial relationship. Should they ever try to converse at a deeper level, it will always end in a lot of barking and growling.

Dragon finds Dog hostile and unenthusiastic, while Dog turns its nose up on Dragon's grand ambitions and ideals. They do not hold the same values in life and rarely find themselves frolicking along at the same pace. The arrows of antagonism working against them are usually too strong for any serious attraction to arise between them.

Where Dragon and Dog can meet with high compatibility and success is when there is an Ox and a Sheep in the mix. When four such people come together, they form the *Earth Cross* together, a powerful combination that manifests wealth, prosperity and success. So should a Dog and Dragon find themselves ending up as a married couple, if they have an Ox child and a Sheep child together, their family unit, even if not always harmonious, can achieve wealth and success beyond anyone's imagination. In 2020, the feng shui winds blow more kindly on the Dragon and Dog pair, with Dragon enjoying heaven's blessings and Dog benefitting from the *Prosperity Star*.

Both Dog & Dragon are feeling ambitious this year, and if they can find a way to work together where each bring different talents to the table, their collaboration can be successful.

Dog and Dragon make better friends than lovers, and they can become good time friends if they keep each other at arm's length. They enjoy holidaying together and can even work on the same team, but will always need the presence of others to dissolve the tension that's bound to build up if it is just the two of them.

CURE: If Dog and Dragon are already married, display the **Earth Cross Mirror** in the home you share together to bring in the energies of the Ox and Sheep. This transforms the negative energies that bounce off each other into positive ones.

DOG/SNAKE *unbalanced*

Lopsided match, but some chemistry in 2020

Dog and Snake have little natural affinity unless there is a common interest binding them together. Both being genial types, this relationship can well work on the surface, but theirs will be a pairing contingent on many other factors, and should these factors disappear, so will their love and need for each other.

Dog is loyal to a fault and will often follow its partner to the ends of the earth, but a Snake partner may well make this difficult. Snake is a loner while Dog adores company, and so the dissimilarities start. Snake often misinterprets Dog's devotion as neediness, and eventually the Dog will lose interest. One can only stay constant and faithful for so long if the feelings never get reciprocated.

In 2020, Snake shows more interest in the Dog, so it is highly possible that should the two meet, something could start up between them. And for this year at least, the passion they share will be real.

But the question will be whether this match can last. Because they lack natural affinity, it will be hard work, especially on the part of the Dog. Snake is often the more ambitious of the two, and this could end up being a bone of contention. Snake starts to feel that Dog is holding it back; Dog feels Snake is emphasizing the wrong things in life. Neither finds it easy to see eye to eye on many issues.

Their lifestyle tastes are also quite different. Snake likes to be pampered and almost requires five-star creature comforts all the way, while Dog is happy and sometimes even prefers to rough it out. Snake appreciates the fine arts and classical music, Dog often prefers slapstick comedy. In bringing up kids, the Snake parent is far more attentive, something that could well go against Dog's core beliefs, that children should toughen up by being allowed to fail and make their own mistakes.

Because Dog and Snake are so different in attitudes and outlooks, theirs is a poor match for marriage. As friends and work mates, they get along fine, but when a deeper commitment or connection is attempted, they are likely to fight.

2020 sees a good time between these two signs, but if you are thinking of taking things to the next level, be very sure before taking that leap of faith.

DOG/HORSE ***blissful***

Astrological allies enjoying sum-of-ten luck

A wonderful pairing in every way! Dog and Horse are astrological allies, belonging to the *Trinity of Adventurers* together with the Tiger. They share similar interests and have compatible personalities. Both are rather sensible and rational types.

With Dog and Horse, there is rarely any quarrelling because both prefer to agree than disagree. There is marvellous cooperation and communication between them, and even when Horse occasionally gets restless, its Dog partner understands and does not interfere.

In a Dog-Horse pairing, neither will try to dominate or compete with the other, and their affinity makes them trust each other implicitly. They are mindful never to do anything that could be conceived as hurtful to one another, so there is an abundance of compassion, empathy and goodwill in this relationship.

Should a Dog and Horse get married, theirs will be a home filled with love and laughter that comprises not just their immediate family unit, but extended family

★★★★★

and friends as well. Both Dog and Horse are sociable creatures and love to entertain, so it will not be unsual for a Dog-Horse household to transform into a clubhouse of sorts, with friends dropping by regularly to hang out. They both enjoy attending parties, so they make a wonderful society couple.

This year, Dog enjoys one *Big Auspicious* and one *Small Auspicious* star, bringing many new opportunities and joyous occasions its way. Horse meanwhile benefits indirectly from its ally's good fortune, and having a Dog as its partner allows Horse to share in these benefits.

At home, Dog and Horse make a cozy couple, where they cuddle up nicely in each other's arms. If the going gets tough for the Horse, as it might in 2020, a Dog partner instinctively knows what to do to lift Horse's spirits.

Love is always in the air with these two, and while their relationship may start off hot and passionate, it will cool to a comfortable simmer. But the sparks remain, and even when life throws slings and arrows their way, Dog and Horse continually find reasons to rejoice. They have each other's backs, and for both, this is a relationship pairing that is hard to beat.

DOG/SHEEP *earth friends*

Can work out but depends more on Sheep

Sheep could fall quite head over heels for the Dog this year. For both, the year ahead looks very positive where few things go wrong for either, and both are in the mood for love.

Their matching Earth elements put them in beautiful synchronicity, so the attraction could be very strong. Should they meet this year, chances of finding themselves getting into a relationship are high.

Both Dog and Sheep's element luck levels are looking strong in 2020, with very good and excellent indications in most categories. The feng shui winds blowing their way are also compatible, with Dog enjoying great wealth indications and Sheep's networking connections allowing Dog's plans to unfold without hitches.

But the Dog and Sheep pairing tends to be one which can grow strongly co-dependent, which is not always a good thing. Sheep's apparent vulnerability at first brings out all the protective instincts in the Dog. Dog will want to take care of its Sheep mate, and the Sheep will let it. But the more Sheep exploits

Dog's compassionate nature, the more Dog will come to resent Sheep's clingy nature. When this happens, the relationship could start to break down. If Sheep wants the relationship to work out, it needs to actively resist getting drawn into a relationship where it looks towards the Dog for everything.

The Sheep is an independent and highly capable sign, perfectly able to move through life without a partner to meet its every need. When it gets together with a Dog however, it reacts to Dog's willingness to do everything by letting it. However, this backfires because Dog's unabated devotion and dependability does not last.

This can be a happy union, but Sheep has to be ever mindful how it handles its Dog partner, because the Dog, when fed up, can kick its heels and romp away without so much as a backward glance. The longevity of this relationship depends then on how determined the Sheep is at making things work.

Not a fully balanced relationship. Should they break up, the separation will hit the Sheep much harder than the Dog. But if married with children, chances of the union lasting are higher, as the Dog is a family person and will go to great lengths to protect its kin.

DOG/MONKEY ***autumn trinity***

Differing aspirations make this match difficult

Dog and Monkey both belong to the *Seasonal Trinity of Autumn*, so for them, they find wealth together in the season of autumn, particularly if they have a Rooster in the mix. For Dog and Monkey, they can thus make money together, so in commercial ventures, their energies blend extremely well.

In 2020, both enjoy good feng shui winds, with Dog leading the charge with the *Prosperity Star.* Monkey's *Peach Blossom* energies meanwhile make it extremely attractive to the Dog, so romance could well blossom between these two. And should they get together, they enjoy a good year together.

Dog admires Monkey's creativity and genius, while Monkey appreciates Dog's loyalty and steadfastness. Together they can lead a happy co-existence, but there is unlikely to be much passion of the exhilarating kind. Theirs will be a rather bland combination, where neither will rile or upset the other too much, but where they do not conjure up great excitement either. In a marriage between Monkey and Dog, Monkey naturally jumps in to take the lead and Dog will usually follow. But in 2020,

 ★★★

Dog's luck is superior to Monkey's, and Dog may not make such a willing follower. If there is any tussle for control, things could get growlier than usual, but even if they do fight, their quarrels never rise to a temperature beyond repair.

While Dog and Monkey can get along, their personalities and attitudes are quite different. Work and personal achievement takes up much of Monkey's thoughts, and a Dog partner will simply not share the same level of enthusiasm.

When pursuing a big goal or aspiration, Monkey will look for someone to bounce ideas off, but Dog is unlikely to provide a suitable sounding board. And so Monkey could go in search of its intellectual match elsewhere, and should that person make a play for the Monkey, Monkey could well succumb.

Dog strives for a happy, safe and comfortable home life, and cannot understand when Monkey wants to risk everything for a marginal improvement in living standards. If their ambitions diverge too drastically, it is the easiest thing for Monkey to swing into the arms of another, leaving its Dog partner dumbfounded and devastated. Can work, but if it doesn't, Dog will tend to be on the losing end.

DOG/ROOSTER *autumn friends*

A lot of genuine love here

The Dog and Rooster have the potential to form a very happy pairing despite their differing personalities and divergent world views, as they inspire a great deal of genuine love for one another.

Dog accepts the imperiousness of Rooster and as a result, goes beneath the skin of this proud individual and brings out some of its finest qualities. Rooster appreciates Dog's loyalty and thus forgives it its occasional holier than thou outbursts. They may not live by the same standards of morality, but they do respect each other's individuality and viewpoints.

In a marriage, these two individuals are quite capable of leading their own lives and doing their own thing but they also come together for the important occasions. They are unlikely to grow apart as their bonds do tend to grow stronger with the passing years.

Dog will often be in awe of Rooster's capabilities, as a result of which Dog willingly endures the pontifications of the Rooster. Dog identifies with Rooster's high ideals and quest for perfection, so is both understanding and tolerant. There are more than enough ingredients therefore for a happy match.

 ★★★★

In 2020, Dog's element luck levels are high compared to those of Rooster, so it will be Dog that takes charge for a change. Rooster continues to have all the ideas and opinions, but when it comes to taking action, it will be Dog leading the charge. And for once, Rooster will happily follow.

Dog and Rooster are also seasonal friends belonging to the *Trinity of Autumn* with the Monkey. Should Dog and Rooster be together, having a Monkey child brings their family a lot of prosperity luck.

In business, if Dog and Rooster are in partnership, introducing a Monkey gives a big boost to wealth luck. This can also be done symbolically, by displaying a Monkey together with Rooster and Dog in the office to activate this aspect of wealth luck.

In 2020, Dog and Rooster enjoy a enviable year, both sharing a *Big Auspicious Star* and very good feng shui winds. A lot of happiness and success for this pair.

DOG/DOG *happiness*

Meeting with much success together in 2020

Two Dogs live harmoniously together. They are neither competitive nor judgemental with each other, each respecting each other's personal space, aspirations and eccentricities. When two Dogs get together, they soon find their respective comfort levels and even their own corners in the home, and then there should be continuing harmony in their domestic household.

Dog people are usually sensitive to their spouse and also considerate as individuals, so it is unlikely for them to have any major differences of opinion. When a Dog marries another Dog, they tend to bring out all the more congenial aspects of the other's personality.

Two Dogs where both are the same age will see any extra high or extra low energies caused by element interactions during the year eliciting sympathy and help from the other. And where one side is twelve years older or younger, the younger will give way to the older. This is a natural instinct of Dog people, as they are usually respectful of age. Dogs respect traditional values and can be wary of changes taking place too fast, so two Dogs in a partnership will tend to be extra careful.

★★★★

Dogs are social animals, so two Dogs together will have energy levels that match each other's when it comes to adventure, travel and socialising. Two Dogs will always enjoy a good party, so they could well become society's It couple. They are also not overly precious, able to enjoy both the very glam and the more down-to-earth occasions. They never complain and they get along very well.

In 2020, the Dog enjoys some truly spectacular luck, with very good element luck indications as well as the *Prosperity Star* in its sector. Two Dogs working together bring double the success, so there will be many mutual celebrations to be had should they join forces. They can look forward to a very successful year financially, with not just good feng shui winds but also the 24 Mountains Constellation bringing them *Big and Small Auspicious* luck.

Two Dogs make for a happy and lasting couple, and in 2020, some windfall opportunities as well!

DOG/BOAR ***soulmates***

An enduring couple having a great year!

Dog and Boar are soulmates of the Zodiac, forming the *House of Domesticity* together. In a marriage, they build the happiest of homes together, and love nothing more than to nurture their brood and watch them grow. While both Dog and Boar individually can be industrious, with each other, their thoughts turn to the simpler joys of life, so these two make a better pair in love than in work.

Both Dog and Boar know how to enjoy life, and neither will allow everyday stresses and strains to get them down. Few things cause the Dog to lose sight of the things that make existence meaningful, and the same goes for the Boar. Whether they are doing well financially or not, they find a way to live beyond their means, and their source of happiness is rarely tied to the size of their bank accounts.

In 2020, both Dog and Boar enjoy superlative wealth luck. They have the *Prosperity Star* on their side, so money should not be a problem for them.

As a pair, each are likely to be financially independent, and when they are, both tend to be generous when it comes to spoiling loved ones and family. They have the same mindset towards money, giving priority to enjoyment now rather than saving up for the future. It is one way to live, and in a year when both are doing well, one can expect a Dog-Boar household to be a lavish experience in 2020.

While Dog and Boar may not make for an insanely passionate couple, they share a love of a much more long-lasting kind. They are tender towards one another, and for those with kids, a lot of their focus will go into bringing up their children.

Children of Dog-Boar families will have both parents firmly influencing their lives. Whether one or both parents work, both will make it a point to have an active hand at parenting. The Dog and Boar pair usually places a lot more weight on happiness than on wealth, and because their aspirations align so closely, they never have reason to fight over what often bothers other couples.

Whether they live in a castle or a cave, Dog and Boar always find a way to be happy together. And in 2020, they don't need to look very hard for ways, because they have all the money they need to fulfill most of their worldly desires.

CHAPTER 6

DOG'S MONTH BY MONTH LUCK FOR 2020

OVERVIEW FOR THE DOG 2020

Big & Small Auspicious luck indications hold out a lot of promise

Those born under the Dog sign can look forward to countless wonderful developments this coming year! The energies of the ruling animal sign, the Rat, combines with those of the Dog to bring the *Ho Tu* of 3/8. This suggests all Dog sign individuals enjoy great leadership and command, and those in charge of others will wield wise and benevolent influence over their charges.

> The Dog's element luck is strong this year, giving you the inner confidence to make astute and definitive decisions. A year when you can seize back the initiative to take your life in whatever direction you prefer.

There's very little to get in the way of your success apart from temporary time afflictions, so you can move resolutely forward with your plans with confidence. This year you find others leaning on you for support rather than the other way around; and yet the more you help others, the more help you receive in return. The Dog has always been the loyal and genuine kind, and this year, you see many of your own positive traits mirrored in the way others respond to you. The more generous you are, the more generous others are towards you. The more you give, the more you receive. The 24 Mountains also brings excellent indications your way, with a *Small Auspicious* and *Big Auspicious*. Big Auspicious comes from the direction of the Rooster, so working with a Rooster-born, your seasonal friend, bodes well indeed.

In 2020, look out for ways to expand your horizons and to accumulate new knowledge. There's so much in the world to explore and you haven't seen a fraction of it yet. The more you open your mind, the more opportunities will come your way; and you start recognising more of these as the big breaks you've been waiting for.

Indeed, the world is your oyster! The **38 year old Water Dog** in particular can look forward to suddenly coming into seriously big money. But it will not be just in monetary terms that the Dog excels, it is a fulfilling year all round where you experience memorable moments that enrich your life and cause you to grow and develop as a person.

The Dog's best months this year are March, May, August, September, October and December.

FIRST Month

February 4th - March 5th 2020

Year starts on a strong note. Be bold!

The year begins as it means to continue, on a high note! You're in a great mood and on your own unique level when it comes to energy and drive. Very little holds you back this month. In fact you're so self-confident that you tend to ignore opinions and remarks offered that don't align well with your own. You're absolutely correct to avoid wet blankets who want to rain on your parade, but some may have genuine knowledge or suggestions to impart. Don't sweep everyone aside with the same brush stroke.

Wealth luck is promising, both current and future wealth, making this an excellent time for new investments. But when you're doing well, don't start to scrimp and save. When you spend or give away money, you make room for more to come into your life.

The danger this month is to act without thinking. The Dog is usually a wonderfully thoughtful person, but your focus on the more material aspects of life could cause you to momentarily forget your manners.

No harm done, you just have to learn to apologise if you slight or overlook anyone in your haste and hurry.

ENHANCER: The Dog benefits from the **Element Balancing Amulet** to ensure your good fortune does not tip into imbalance. Your world is fast-paced right now, which could cause you to miss rare opportunities that come along. This amulet helps bring your elements back into check, allowing you to make the most of your good fortune luck.

Work & Career - *Promotion luck*

A profitable month when you enjoy upward mobility and glide up the corporate ladder with ease. You get on famously with everyone from colleagues to subordinates to powerful personages. You talk well and convincingly, and your relationships are scaling new heights. Make the most of this time to solidify friendships and to secure the loyalty of the key people you work with.

Business - *New ideas*

As you toss ideas around, you may hit on what you think must be a definite winner. Don't be impulsive. Time is on your side, so use it well. Do not make rash decisions. If you have good ideas, allow them time to take shape.

Analyse everything thoroughly before setting any big plan into motion.

Relationships - *Riding high*

Passion rules and there's much to make your heart race! Expect opportunities and follow your heart. If you have responsibilities, make a conscious effort not to neglect them. This month can be deceptive because you're riding a chart filled with lucky stars. Be as outrageous as you want, but don't do anything you'll regret later.

Friends & Family - *Avoid gossip*

It may be tempting to indulge in harmless gossip with an old friend, but don't get sucked into a destructive spiral of analysis paralysis. Keep touchy subjects out of conversations with friends, no matter how close they may be. You may find yourself in a situation where pals think they are helping you, but really they are interfering with your family life. Don't let them. It may rock the boat.

Education - *Awards & accolades*

The young Dog benefits from the turbo-charged energies of the month. You do well academically as well as in your extracurricular activities. This month could see you receive a meaningful award. Success comes to those who set their sights high.

SECOND Month

March 6th - April 4th 2020

Wealth & success luck gets doubled

Fabulous luck awaits you! Success is written all over your chart. You have many brilliant ideas up your sleeve, but pursuing too many may see you spreading yourself too thin. It is better to focus on one big thing and put your entire focus on it to make it a stunning success. Mediocrity has no place with you this month; it is all or nothing.

Go for goal. Don't set targets that compromise. You know just where you want to get to, so set your mind to getting there. If you let yourself get side-tracked, this will turn out to be just like any other month, but this period you can really achieve great things, so stay focused.

If you set your expectations high, you can succeed beyond even your own wildest dreams! No goal is too big for you at this time. If you have to, rope others in to help you. You have a great deal of influence, so use it. Exercise your leadership to get others on board. Don't do things by half measures and don't limit yourself by trying to be a one-man show.

Work & Career - *All-consuming*

You are happiest when working on a project that consumes you, and this month you may be put in charge of something truly important, something that gives you the chance to make your mark and showcase your worth. But you may find it eating into your personal time. If you don't have a family to worry about, you'll probably be absolutely blissed out by the experience. But those with lives other than your work may have to make some sacrifices.

Business - *Turning thoughts to the future*

Business luck is terrific. As well as focusing on immediate sales, this is a good time to think towards the future. Longer term initiatives kick-started now tend to pan out well. Something could catch your attention that completely re-energizes you. An unexpected call could lead to a special mission that has incredible knock-on effects on your business and income. Operationally, your outfit will run just fine, leaving you time to strategize and pursue new things.

You may find yourself venturing into the unknown with some of the new initiatives you'll be taking on. Don't let them intimidate you; instead, let them invigorate you. What you need is to be motivated into thinking big, because the bigger you think, the bigger the rewards.

Relationships - *Good news*

This month brings good news in matters of the heart. You can look forward to good times ahead, and this is true for both the single and attached Dog. Be open about your affections. If there's something you want to say, blurt it out. Holding it in could cost you a whole truckload of loving! For some, you may be ready to take your relationship a step further. This is an auspicious time for marriage proposals, weddings and renewal of vows. Voicing your feelings will reaffirm them and make your union stronger.

Family - *Important*

Family plays a big part in your life now. There are many opportunities for family reunions, and all make your family bonds stronger. Your spouse could do a complete turnaround and crave the company of your folks more than you do yourself! You find yourself surprisingly pleased with this, and it could sweeten and strengthen your marriage.

Education - *Excelling*

Everything is aligned for you to excel, so take every opportunity to shine. Don't think of yourself as good in certain subjects. You can be brilliant at everything!

THIRD Month

April 5th - May 5th 2020

Robbery star warns of being conned

This month is peppered with potholes. You're targeted by friends and foes alike; friends who are jealous and foes who covet what you have. The best thing to do is keep a low profile. Try not to draw attention to yourself. Avoid seeking out publicity. At work, be a team player, but don't make any overt leadership plays. Others won't look kindly on this, no matter how well intentioned. Avoid speculation, gambling and risk-taking. Spending money is quite a good way to avoid losing it, because you need to create a flow; may be the excuse you've been looking for you to hit the shops!

CURE: There is indication of financial or material loss through theft, robbery or being cheated. Carry the **Rhino and Elephant Anti-Burglary Amulet** to counter these loss energies.

Work & Career - *Correcting mistakes*

You meet with several sticky situations at work. If something goes wrong that is obviously your fault, it may be easiest to stand and face the music, but unfortunately it won't be as straight forward as that. You may have to think through all repercussions. But while you should not dodge responsibility, think about what you can do to fix things. No one wants an apology that leads to no solution. If you're serious about the longevity of your position, start exercising those brain muscles and think outside the box.

Business - *Consolidate*

This is a time for consolidation. Hold off investment or expansion plans till next month if you can. If things are going well, maintain the status quo. Manage your finances carefully or you could find yourself spending more than you can afford. Not a time to take chances. Err on the side of caution when spending money. If you don't get greedy, nothing untoward will happen. Avoid important meetings. Your luck is down, and in a year when you have so many good months, try to plan your schedule so you fix important discussions in months when luck is on your side.

Relationships - *Plateau*

You may feel like you're stuck in limbo when it comes to relationships. Whether its your own indecisiveness putting a hold on things, or your partner who is the culprit does not make any difference. Don't struggle over something you cannot change. Develop some patience and see where the tide takes you. Things resolve themselves soon enough. Keeping things as they are could actually be quite comforting because you are not ready for the next stage of the relationship, even if you think you are.

Friendships - *Natural joy*
Friendships may suffer from misunderstandings. Avoid contentious subjects because the people around you tend to be more thin-skinned than usual. If someone can't take a joke, don't tease them. There are times when you are fragile too, so be understanding. The more supportive you are of your pals, the more they will want you around them.

Education - *Emotional*
Study luck is average, although the quality of your work may be influenced by what's on your mind rather than actual abilities. Avoid complicating things by dating - it has the potential to mess with you emotionally. You may want to spend more time with your parents and family, who will be your pillars of strength this month.

FOURTH Month

May 6th - June 5th 2020

Heaven luck smiling on you. So many opportunities to shine!

A happy month when things fall nicely into place. You don't need to do too much to secure success in whatever you have your hands in. Others rush to your aid and you are in no shortage of allies and admirers. What's even more exciting is the presence of someone important who becomes a bigger part of your life as the months unfolds.

They have the power and influence to swing something big in your favour, and like you enough to delight in the good news it brings. Nurture this relationship; this person is unlikely to be a fly-by-night acquaintance, but one who can become a true friend and mentor for a long time to come.

Your connections with others plays a big role in your success. Fit in one-to-one meetings to cement new friendships. Someone in a good position to help could take you under their wing. Welcome this and work at nurturing such a relationship.

TIP: The Dog benefits from carrying the **Gui Ren Amulet** to activate mentor and benefactor luck; more than what you know is who you know. You can also carry your **Guardian Bodhisattva Amitabha** who ensures no obstacles arise. The month holds out a lot of promise. Calling on celestial assistance helps ensure you make the most of your good fortune luck of the moment, and perhaps even secure your big break!

Work & Career - *Impressive*

You have everything from job satisfaction to promotion luck. Your biggest advantage will be having the decisions makers at the top completely behind you. Work at becoming close to them, and impress them not just with your ways with words, but with first-rate work and results. Your productivity goes into overdrive and your objectives are easily met with time to spare. This month you find it easy to show the people who matter what you can really do. Everyone seems to think all the good things are due entirely to you. Enjoy your achievements but no harm sharing credit with the team.

Business - *Big deals*

Wealth luck has never been better. Sealing big deals and winning major contracts are all possible now, so be ambitious when pitching for jobs. Do not think too small. You're riding a wave of success and if you want to ride it well, quit your conservative streak and show a bit of grit and courage. This is a good time to embark on new ventures in new directions, and to inject more creative flair into what you do.

Love & Relationships - *Feeling sociable*

You're happier and bubblier than usual, making you wildly attractive! Your energetic spark is extremely contagious and you find the people around you perking up to match your vivacious mood. If single, you are happiest flirting with a number of potential suitors rather than developing a relationship with a single person. Have fun. No need to settle down just yet.

Education - *Wise words*

Your capacity for learning new things seems limitless and so is your vision for the future. A relaxing and fun filled time when you enjoy all your subjects and learning becomes fun. Accept wise words offered by your elders. They hold more wisdom than you at first realise.

FIFTH Month

June 6th - July 6th 2020

Hitting a bumpy patch. Five Yellow arrives.

A month best spent lying low. The *Five Yellow* warns of impending obstacles, so avoid taking risks. If you are lucky, this month will turn out dull and uneventful. Try not to attract too much attention to whatever successes come your way, or you could instigate jealousy from others. There may be minor disappointments to face, and after the ease of last month, this one could feel rather bumpy. Get yourself the **Evil Eye Anti Jealousy Amulet.**

WOFS™

Some of you may encounter problems from excessive gossiping. Avoid rumour-mongering and resist the temptation of a spectacular retort. Best let any gossip die a natural death. You can say something to brush it aside, but don't start your own malicious tale or it will definitely boomerang.

The most important things now are to avoid big risks, watch your finances, and ensure the feng shui of your home and office are properly covered so you don't succumb to avoidable bad luck. People may let you down, road bumps appear out of nowhere, but this is all temporary. Your luck improves next month.

CURE: Carry the **Five Element Pagoda Amulet**, and install one in your home sector of NW. You can also wear the **colour white**; this will help exhaust the malevolent Earth energies of the *wu wang*.

Work & Career - *Dog eats dog*

One of those months where when something can go wrong, it does. Don't let your guard down, especially those working in office environments where rivalry between staff is endemic and sometimes destructive. It could be a matter of survival of the fittest, so get yourself into the frame of mind to fight if you have to. You come out in one piece whatever happens, because while you have some unlucky stars, you have the mental strength to battle through whatever crises you meet up with. But life at the office will not be a walk in the park. Brace yourself, make friends rather than enemies, and keep your head down.

Business - *Lie low*

Overall business luck may be good this year, but take caution this month. Be alert to changes in the business environment. Don't go by instincts alone when making decisions. Try to be as informed as you can when deciding on important issues. You may have a lot on your mind, but this is not the time to speak out, especially if what you have to say could be radical or unpopular. Keeping the status quo is the best way to maintain your luck through this patchy time.

Relationships - *Confidante*

Things could be better when it comes to romance, but this aspect of your life brings you more joy than work matters right now. Even if you have the odd misunderstanding with your partner, you resolve things quickly, especially if you rope them in as confidante to your other problems. As for dating, you're not likely to be in the mood to meet new people.

Education - *Tricky friendships*

Schoolwork is something of a chore. Some friendships may get tricky, especially if there's a someone new in the picture. Relationship dynamics feature in your life right now, and probably occupy more of your thoughts than they should. Save time for focused attention on your schoolwork and you will find it easier to cope.

SIXTH Month

July 7th - Aug 7th 2020

Good time to explore new frontiers

Your luck improves, especially when it comes to socializing, romancing and developing friendships. You are in good spirits and others enjoy being around you. A good time to take up a new hobby or learn a new skill. You could find a whole new way of enjoying yourself. You have career luck on your side, and if willing to make radical changes, you may be setting yourself up for a big promotion.

There's no limit to what you can achieve now, especially when it involves your creativity and imagination. Students enjoy great study luck, and anyone involved in writing and the literary fields will see success come easily.

Work & Career - *Inspired*

Make full use of your creativity. Pitch ideas regularly and keep thinking on your toes. Once you open the floodgates to creativity, you have so much to offer. If you are in a dead-end job that is beginning to bore you, it may be time to move on. But think through big decisions carefully before you make them, because once you make up your mind there is no turning back.

Business - *A period of growth*

Dogs have a good time ahead. You are filled with so many good ideas waiting to be implemented! While you can't pursue all of them at once, you enjoy fantastic ally luck, and partners with potential could materialize, offering you ways to expand with less capital and less risk. Effective delegation will also free yourself up to spend more time on the strategic aspects of your business. You have some good staff on your team and if you need new hires, go ahead and hire! This is a promosing time for expansion and growth.

Don't shun advice given by others. Tap the brains of those with something to teach you. You may be surprised at who ends up giving you the best tips and tricks. When advice is offered, listen. Don't be arrogant.

Love & Relationships - *Don't hold back*

The Dog is feeling more romantic than usual, so when it comes to love, don't hold back! Wear your heart on your sleeve if you must - you have little to lose! People fall in love with the true you, so don't be shy about revealing the real you. There's no need to play games or drag out the courting period. If you've met the one who sets your heart on fire, make your move! You have the luck of the *Peach Blossom* firmly on your side.

Friendships - *Bring opportunities*

Friends count for a lot this month. This is no time to be a homebody. Socialising with those who count as your pals enriches your life in all its different aspects. Whether you gain ideas for work, find a buddy to share a laugh with, or need advice on relationship matters, your friends are there for you. Holing up at home will stifle your creativity and you could miss out on opportunities meant for you. Occasionally, throw a dinner party for friends, or invite your business associates round. Get the whole family involved in entertaining. Your invitees will appreciate your effort, and who knows what it could lead to!

Education - *Pursue what interests you*

Everything goes well for the young Dog in school. This month sees you grow in confidence. Pursue whatever is of interest to you. Don't worry too much about the academic side. Results come if you put the work in; building a well-rounded you is more important now.

SEVENTH Month

Aug 8th - Sept 7th 2020

Quarrelsome but others listen to you

You are afflicted by the quarrelsome star, which makes you difficult to work with. But you have the Natural Leader *Ho Tu* on your side due to your combination of stars. This helps you retain influence despite your irritable mood and bad temper. Make an effort to hold that temper in check. If you can divert your "anger" energies to more productive uses, the month holds a lot of promise.

The Dog wields power arising from the *Ho Tu* in your chart. If you can keep the *Quarrelsome Star* from taking over your mood, you make an effective leader, and can lead your team to notable success.

ENHANCER: Carry the **Ho Tu Enhancer** to boost the auspicious aspects of your luck this month. The **Dragon Horse** or **Chi Lin** is also an effective symbol to bring out the powers of the Ho Tu.

Work & Career - *Employ some tact*

Career luck is good, especially for those in managerial positions. Your hot blood keeps you efficient and on-the-ball, but don't let it make you a nuisance. Channel your dominant energy towards work. Keep in mind your mouth is probably not your best asset at this time. When engaging in group discussion, watch the tone you use when you contribute. There's always more than one way to say the same thing. Adopt more tact in your language and you will find yourself a lot more effective.

Business - *Competition on the horizon*

There is indication of much fiercer competition than you're used to, but you prevail and come out triumphant if you can maintain your confidence. You may not win every battle, but you will win the war. Always take the longer-term view when looking for results. Don't trade long-term success for a quick buck. Your luck has a long arc this year; play that arc. Resist fraternizing with the enemy lest you let on too much or lose your cool in conversation.

When dealing with associates and business partners, carry the **Apple Peace Amulet** to keep the temperature of discussions down. In your excitement, your bark may get a bit too loud, giving others the wrong idea.

Relationships - *Mood swings*
Romance fizzles out due to your irritable mood. You are still loveable, but less so. Your mood swings may put people off, especially those who may not know you well. And you yourself may be undecided what you want.

Parts of you need company to banter or even quarrel with, but when the quarrel heats up, it gets everyone involved upset. You need to work at being a better companion if you want good companionship back. If you're looking for romance, you to have to do a lot to earn it this month!

Education - *Take a break from social media*
Things may be a little tough for the young Dog because the quarrelsome energies that surround you make it difficult. Try not to get worked up over issues. Conflict with friends could get you down.

Don't put too much importance on what others think. If it helps, spend more time focused on schoolwork rather than your popularity. Stay away from social media if that's getting you down. Look for a new hobby to try your hand at; it will take your mind of the things that may be bothering you, but that really shouldn't.

EIGHTH Month

Sept 8th - Oct 7th 2020

Finding shortcuts to overcome deflated energy levels.

You may not be as bright and perky as usual, and your sense of humour may be a little slower to shine through courtesy of the troublesome *Illness Star.* But while the #2 may be making you feel less energetic, you do have amazing indications with the *sum-of-ten.* This brings completion luck, as well as new and lucrative opportunities. Don't let your flagging energy levels hold you back. Get help, work in teams, learn to delegate and find more efficient ways to do the same work.

This might be the time to start letting go of responsibilities you previously clung on to. If you want to grow, you need to trust others to assist you where they can, so you can pursue new pastures and scout out new opportunities.

Learn to be a boss and to share rewards. You need help, so don't try to do everything yourself.

TIP: Carry the **Anti Illness Amulet** to counter the illness energies this month. The **38 year old Water Dog** especially should take more care of health issues. Don't let illness and poor health hamper your positive luck indications.

Work & Career - *Don't get careless*

You find yourself easily distracted. Getting enough sleep could prove a problem, and this makes you less productive at work the next day. Rearrange your lifestyle so you get enough rest as you are physically weaker. You have good opportunities, but a lack of ability to focus could cost you your "big break".

Watch out for careless mistakes. If you are involved in tedious work, it is easy to slip up. Try not to make too many blunders or your ratings with the boss could slide. Your overall luck however is good, so you have nothing to worry about in the longer term. The negative aspects of the month are transient in nature. Just hang on tight and ride out this low energy period.

Business - *Negotiate another time*

Wealth luck is good and your success will be riding

on that. Focus on collection of money. You haven't made the sale till the cheque clears. Not a good idea to schedule too many important meetings, as fatigue may cloud your judgement. Leave important negotiations to another time. Better to focus on improving internal processes than have too many dealings with outsiders. Those working in industries where risk of injury is high should be more careful. Take steps to minimize risk, as risk of injury is higher with the #2 star hovering.

Relationships - *Cosying up at home*

Those attached will enjoy spending quiet time bonding with their partner but won't be in the mood for socialising or meeting new people. You don't have the energy to party. Don't feel pressured to show up if you're not feeling up to it. You can always make it up to your friends another time.

Education - *Watch deadlines*

A low energy month for the Dog, which means your attention span is probably shorter and you lack inspiration and motivation. Start your assignments early so you don't have to complete in a panic when the work becomes due. Don't let deadlines creep up on you.

NINTH Month

Oct 8th - Nov 6th 2020

Victory luck on your side. Beating the competition.

The *Victory Star* brings plenty of wealth and new opportunities your way! Your buoyant energy returns, putting you in a good position to make the most of your current advantages. But while the month looks promising, it also brings fierce competition and jealousy from others. As your success grows, so do the number of envious eyes cast your way.

Kill with kindness and share your good fortune whenever possible. Deal with the competition with clever strategy. No need to become hostile with rivals; you have the influence and ability to make people listen, and you can use this to win people onto your side. If they can't beat you, they may as well join you.

Whether focused on career, family, education or love, there's tons to keep you busy. This month sees more ingredients added to your already hectic life. All the new goings-on you find yourself involved in will be perfect outlets for your surplus energy.

TIP: The Dog should carry the **Victory Banner Amulet** to bring the *Victory Star* in your chart to life. This month is all about winning and getting ahead of the competition. You have the ability now to build up a meaningful lead against your rivals, one that will last some time. Energize the NW of your home and office with the **Windhorse** and by filling this part of the home with activity and use. Keep music playing in this corner.

Victory Banner Amulet

Work & Career - *Happier when leading*

It's all systems go and the more work you get, the happier you are. You are in leadership mode and will tend to try and take charge, whether it is your place to do so or not. Stepping on other people's toes may become your modus operandi; watch you don't upset the wrong person. If you're not leading the team you are working with, it is better you work alone. Taking direct orders is not something you do well in your current frame of mind. Don't break the rules too often though, or Management won't put up with it no matter how good you are. Talent alone is not enough; attitude is more important. Keep the right posture and you can make real progress in your career.

Business - *Cutting deals*

Your abilities to lead are enhanced so use this as a chance to motivate and galvanize your staff. If heading a large company, dedicate time to getting to know all your employees, not just the ones working directly under you. Also a good time to talk business with potential partners and investors. You're convincing when you speak, and cutting a good deal will be easy at this time.

Relationships - *Newer pastures*

Forget about things that happened in the past. Focus on the present. This month love can blossom if you will let it. Seize the initiative and forge ahead onto newer pastures if you've recently ended something. No need to look back. If a relationship has come to a natural end, don't let yourself be talked into rekindling embers that are hardly worth saving. Move on!

Education - *Soaking it up*

Most suitable time for self-improvement and soaking up all the knowledge your teachers have been trying to impart. Your powers of concentration are phenomenal now, so make use of them. The key is motivation and you are your own best motivator when you put your mind to it.

TENTH Month

Nov 7th - Dec 6th 2020

All systems go! Feeling enthusiastic!

A wonderfully energetic month! You're feeling upbeat about everything, and this makes your company much sought after. The Dog sign makes a wonderful pal when happy, knowing just how to lift the spirits of everyone who crosses its path. This month sees you making new friends and forming connections that prove life-long in nature. All aspects of your life will be geared towards your interactions with people and how well you get along with them. Definitely a time when "who you know" trumps "what you know".

A fast-moving month when tapping on connections makes things happen more quickly for you. Success in store. A time for switching into high gear on your projects, moving them out of idea stage into full-fledged implementation.

Things in love move just as quickly as in work. You find new romantic liaisons moving quickly from casual dating into serious commitment. If you've found someone you're sure of, don't play the waiting game too long. A time when long-term commitments work out well. Settling down could be a big draw for the Dog this month and will make you very happy. Don't be averse to settling down.

Work & Career - *Fast-moving*

You get swept up with the sheer pace of things that you may forget to notice the little details. A successful month awaits and those who continue to keep both the small and big picture in mind will leapfrog those who go with the flow. Luck is good; but if you seize that luck and use it to your advantage, it can be great!

This month the effort you put in brings results that are more than proportionate. Worthwhile trying that bit harder if you're serious about making meaningful progress in your career.

Business - *Courage*

Boldness brings bold results. A month that favours the brave. If you know what direction you'd like to move in, put effort into crystallizing your strategy, then move ahead full steam. Once you make up your mind on something, there is no need to seek out or listen to too many opinions. Doing so with the wrong people will only stall you and waste valuable time. This month is lucky for starting things, so if you have the plans and framework already in place, get going. Trust your instincts.

Relationships - *First rate*

If you're single and want to get hitched, get moving with your search. Don't be hesitant or coy. If you are already dating, you may want to take things to the next level. A good month for the Dog to get engaged, married or more involved, so you can move ahead with plenty of peace of mind!

Education - *Work hard play hard*

The young Dog does well in school. Many routes to success this month, whether broadening your knowledge base or deepening it. Your enhanced energy levels allow you to tailor your study methods to you own taste and still find success easily. Call on the help of friends when you need. A time when friendships are important, and strong connections with good company will boost your success. A time to work hard and play hard.

ELEVENTH Month

Dec 7th 2020 - Jan 5th 2021

Your big chance could come now

Big success awaits the Dog this month! You have two *Auspicious Stars* in your chart this year, one Small, one Big. The energies are aligning so nicely for you, indicating that if you're looking for your big break, the time to go for it is now! The Dog can afford to leap before it looks, so to speak. You are not a sign to back off once you take a stance, and you shouldn't. Certainly not now when your luck is looking so strong and so favourable.

You enjoy all kinds of successes with most things go perfectly right; the few that go wrong are still headed in the right direction! Do not let minor obstacles dent your confidence.

Your good fortune luck is so fantastic you might be forgiven if you start thinking of names for your private plane and ocean-going yacht! If anyone can make it big this month, it is the Dog! Set goals and go for dreams that are fast materializing. Don't get side-tracked by anyone or anything; to do so is to waste your luck.

Work & Career - *Effective*

This month you are eloquent, effective and energizing to boot. You inspire those around you and impress those above you in the corporate suites. You work equally well as a team or in a group environment. Your co-workers seem more eager to please you than their superiors! You are happiest meeting and relating to people rather than being desk-bound. Do lots as long as you can keep up the momentum. You have much to offer and there is everything to gain as the stars are in wonderful alignment for you.

Business - *Midas touch*

Since luck is in your hand, you can even venture into what was forbidden territory. Go into the unknown, act on faith and see what happens. Believe in yourself and your skills even as you step into untested waters. You can invest and take risks this month. Whatever you touch seems to turn to gold! So be courageous.

You have all the physical energy, mental strength and spiritual fortitude to take new ideas forward and see them to fruition. Initiatives launched last month begin to bear fruit and you foresee a bountiful harvest! Don't fret at minor obstacles that pop up every now and then. Enjoy the ride!

Relationships - *Be open*
When it comes to loving, there are good times ahead. Be open about your feelings. Why hide your affections if you care for someone? Let the person know! Be vocal and expressive when dealing with your beloved. The more you communicate and let your partner in on your feelings, the more satisfying your love life.

Friends & Family - *Reunions*
Lots of opportunities for family reunions which go really well. There's no fear of relatives picking fights or bickering over petty issues. It is like one big happy family. At such gatherings of the clan, you may even begin to enjoy the company of that cranky uncle or snooty aunt!

Education - *The whole package*
You have amazing potential to shine. You are noticed by teachers not just because of your academic achievements but also your other activities. Put time into school work but also leave time for pursuing other interests. You have the ability to present as the whole package, and this month you can build on all facets of your skills and potential. A rewarding month for the young Dog. The more motivated you can keep yourself, the better you do.

TWELFTH Month

Jan 6th - Feb 3rd 2021

Loss star. Beware jealousies and politics.

The appearance of the *Loss Star* brings danger of money loss, being cheated and even being betrayed. Not an easy month, as after a run of good luck, your fortunes seem to be self-correcting. A time to lie low and to minimize risks. You can lose money easily so avoid investment of any kind; definitely no speculation or gambling since there is no luck in this sector but gaps leading to direct disappearances of money.

Always put safety first and think several steps ahead. Your luck is down so you must use your wits and internal strength to get by. Depend on yourself and don't expect too much help from others. And definitely do not expect goodies to fall into your lap!

You may attract the attention of those envious of what you have. Workplace politics become fierce and unpleasant. Brace yourself and stay out the fray. Play down your achievements and avoid attracting undue attention.

Bhrum Pendant

CURE: Carry the **Anti-Robbery Amulet**. This protects against petty crime but also against others cheating or betraying you. You also need spiritual protection this month. Wear the sacred syllable **Bhrum** to ensure you don't find yourself at the wrong place at the wrong time. This will keep you safe in a month when safety becomes a priority.

Work & Career - *Avoid office wars*

Office politics rears its ugly head. While you may carefully avoid gossiping about others, you cannot prevent others gossiping about you. In such cases, you feel obliged to side with those who seem sympathetic with you. Unfortunately you may be backing the wrong horse! The best thing is not to take obvious sides. If anyone badmouths about you, deny whatever is said and do not retaliate. Play cards close to your chest and confide in no one. Do not mix your professional life with your private one. Tread carefully as the ground seems filled with landmines. Not an auspicious month, so avoid making careless mistakes and do not offend anyone. Having a kind word for everyone and donating some money to charity will help tremendously.

Business - *Obstacles*

Unforeseen problems crop up putting a spoke in the most well-oiled of wheels. Unpredictable obstacles prove frustrating as they delay or scuttle well-laid plans. Don't sign anything big this month. Defer important decisions. Think long rather than short term, as whatever you set in motion now will only bear fruit later. No instant riches this month!

Relationships - *Not a time to do all that much*

Don't put too much hope in budding relationships and you won't get hurt! Not a good time to take your relationship to the next level.

Home & Safety - *Pay attention*

Watch out for danger of your home getting broken into. This risk is possible, so you should place a **Blue Rhino and Elephant** in the Northwest of your home to increase protection against intruders.